"Creativity is an endless parade of possibilities, it's not a goal," Joram Piatigorsky reflects in this diverse collection of essays. Whether writing about the brain, tennis, a bookstore in Iceland, old friends, marriage, death, snow, movies, or the notion of creativity itself, he joins the parade with enthusiasm and unbounded curiosity.

—Bill O'Sullivan,
senior managing editor, *Washingtonian* magazine

"*Truth and Fantasy* hits the mark on so many levels — whether conveying the wisdom of bees or the meaning of fatherhood or the immense power of silence. With a disarming curiosity and warmth, Piatigorsky's observations always emerge plainly, sometimes starkly, in the distance, leaving the reader with a precise and surprising understanding of what is being seen — and even what is not seen. One is reminded constantly of the truism that we are not thinking beings who also feel, but *feeling* beings who also think. These essays, vivid and crisp in their scene-setting and delivery, carry the weight of an immovable foundation upon which we build our lives– with tools and carpentry and right angles, yes, but also – and most important – with magic. *Truth and Fantasy* illuminates that magic. To see it clearly, one need only open the book and turn the page."

—James Mathews,
author of *Last Known Position*

In *Truth and Fantasy: Essays*, Joram Piatigorsky provides widespread insights on numerous topics, always with a nod to imagination. He draws from his family background in fine art

and music, his early life as a California boy devoted to tennis, his career as a research scientist, his collecting Inuit art, his transition from science to writing, his family role as a husband, father and grandfather, and his exotic travels. These well-written, concise essays weave together his thoughts on complementary themes from his extraordinary creative life.

—Stephen S. Lash,
Chairman Emeritus: Christie's

In this captivating compendium of essays, Piatigorsky takes the reader on a metaphysical journey through a variety of subjects. Each vignette is a questioning of the subject's essence and/or dimensions. The piece is a personal accounting, providing a window into the viewpoint of a complex individual, one who is an accomplished lab and field biologist, sportsman, and writer. In these musings, however, Piatigorsky is never dogmatic, but rather provides the reader with a passport to consideration of a topic from that individual's personal context. These analyses of life's landscape stay with you long after you put the book down.

—Margaret McFall-Ngai,
Professor and Director, University of Hawaii at Mānoa,
member National Academy of Sciences U.S.A.

"History and speculation – sometimes correct and sometimes not – contribute to and enable the recognition of creative advances. We are left with this paradox: we advance by looking back." In this perception of Joram Piatigorsky's, we glimmer the motivation of the scientist-cum-writer: not dwelling in reminiscence, but

rather inviting the reader on an expedition. Through concurrent lifetimes dedicated to athletics, research, collecting Inuit and African art, travel and writing, the scientist facilitates our investigation of a life lived large. Then the writer takes over, proposing ways we can weave the truths we have discovered into the fabrics of our own lives.

—John Houston,
Inuit art dealer and filmmaker,
producer of *Atautsikut / Leaving None Behind*

TRUTH AND FANTASY

To Alek — With fondest wishes for a happy + healthy 2022 —

Joram Piatigorsky   12/31/2021

Truth and Fantasy

ESSAYS

by

JORAM PIATIGORSKY

BOOKS

Adelaide Books
New York / Lisbon
2021

TRUTH AND FANTASY: ESSAYS
By Joram Piatigorsky

Published by Adelaide Books, New York / Lisbon
adelaidebooks.org

Editor-in-Chief
Stevan V. Nikolic

For any information, please address Adelaide Books
at info@adelaidebooks.org
or write to:
Adelaide Books
244 Fifth Ave. Suite D27
New York, NY, 10001

ISBN: 978-1-955196-01-7

Printed in the United States of America

Furtwangler, after pleading with the orchestra,

"Gentlemen, this phrase must be – it must –

you know what I mean – please try it again – please,"

said to me at the intermission,

"You see how important it is for a conductor to convey

his wishes clearly?"

(Gregor Piatigorsky, in *Cellist*, p. 126-127)

With gratitude to those who have listened patiently
to my roaming thoughts.

Contents

Author's Note

As a scientist, I conducted experiments designed to find answers to questions that intrigued me in my research on the eye and evolution, and then I linked the results into narratives that made most sense to me. These narratives invariably prompted new questions and broadened my horizons. Finding unexpected relationships between diverse phenomena were most exciting, since they opened novel avenues for study, with new implications to test.

In the present essays, I also ask questions that interest me and consider topics that have been and remain important in my life. I explore the subjects by letting diverse thoughts run freely through my mind. The essays include extensions and rearrangements of selected blogs I have written over the last four years on various subjects that struck my fancy, as well as new essays that fit the themes examined here. The essays are neither comprehensive nor meant to argue a single viewpoint. No absolute answers are ever obtained or even possible; that's not the goal. Rather, I examine relationships between thoughts and observations, which can all be explored further with multiple points of view. I hope these essays stimulate additional thoughts and widen perspectives, as they did for me writing them.

The entire collection of my blogs can be found on my website (joramp.com). One essay, *West Africa: Many Truths Within the Background Noise*, has been previously published with the same title (Adelaide Literary Magazine; May 2019); another, *Defining Moments*, has been modified from its previous publication (*Pondering Proust, Recalling Moments*, Adelaide Literary Award Anthology; 2018; a shortlist winner nominee).

RANDOM THOUGHTS

Nothing to Zero

What are you thinking of?" my friend asked me, when I was sitting silently.

"Nothing," I answered. Then I qualified my response. "Really, nothing."

"Really?" he challenged me, forcing me to wonder whether I *really* had an empty mind, truly absent of thoughts?

I don't think so, I thought. Not really. Even when I sleep, I dream, and when my mind seems blank, I believe some latent thought or feeling is lurking in the crevices, an unconscious "something" related to my life. What an elusive concept, "nothing". Even thinking about "nothing" is a thought, and that's something. Perhaps death is our only exposure to "nothing," but I'm guessing, of course.

Curious, I looked online for information about "nothing". What I found was mostly about the numerical zero. Historically, the Sumerian counting system (where the value of a symbol depended on its relative position) developed 4,000 – 5,000 years ago, but it did not include zero. Zero first appeared in 300 B.C. as a placeholder to designate a space, such as 2025, where the use of a blank space was confusing. The Mayans and Indians independently developed numerical zero before 500 A.D., with the philosophical implications of "nothingness". Later, around

800 A.D., after the concept traveled through China and the Middle East, zero became part of the Arabic number system in Baghdad, and was designated by Arabs as a little, empty circle. It wasn't until the 1600s that zero was used throughout Europe, and now zero is central to physics, engineering, computers, finance and economics.

Fascinating, how zero – "nothing" – went from not existing to central importance in our view of the world. And still signifying nothing.

Since it took thousands of years for humans to think of zero, or "nothing," who would imagine that an animal, much less an invertebrate, could ever develop the concept of "nothing," or even be able to discriminate between less and more? Which brings me to honeybees. James Gorman's article, *Do Bees Know Nothing?,* in the New York Times (June 7, 2018)) reported that bees could not only count, but could also "understand the absence of things…as a numerical quantity: none or zero." Do bees really grasp the concept of "nothing"? Scarlett Howard and Adrian Dyer at the University of Melbourne trained honeybees to recognize the concepts of more or less for a reward and think bees understand the absence of things — shapes on a display in this experiment — as a numerical quantity: none or zero. In brief, Dr. Dyer said the bees "understood that zero was a number lower than one and part of a sequence of numbers."

A number of scientists correctly cautioned against interpreting these findings as if the bees were humans. What goes on in the bee brain, or why a bee does what it does, is beyond our present knowledge. A lot can and did happen in the 500 million years of evolution between a bee and human brain. But, hey, a little humility, please. Bees apparently can be trained to distinguish between the numbers of shape displays, as well as learn from each other and solve problems.

The point here is not to establish what goes on in a bee brain, but rather to show that we must not prematurely discard the idea that something unexpected, and possibly very important, is happening when we're considering a subject that is beyond our present comprehension. We often say "nothing" to substitute for what we don't know. For example, we don't know what most of the genetic material (DNA) does, so we say it's junk DNA, it does "nothing". The amount of DNA doing nothing is decreasing as we learn more about its many functions. We say the endless, seemingly empty, space of the universe is mostly a void with "nothing" in it. Really? We may not see anything (yet), but what's all that mysterious dark matter and dark energy? There's a disorder of feeling anxious when getting up in the morning (called morning anxiety) without knowing why, and "nothing" we know accounts for it. Freud postulated the unconscious – thoughts and feelings that occur without our awareness. Without awareness? Is that "nothing?" Maybe it's poorly regulated nervous activity that needs some synchronization after a night's sleep. "Nothing" is not a satisfactory answer to not knowing.

What appears to be "nothing" may often be a red flag signaling unanswered questions for a basic scientist, or any curious person to seek an answer.

Neutral

Along the line of nothing being something, and except for rare exceptions, I don't believe in the concept of neutral as inconsequential. Everything in my opinion has an effect. Consider the famous butterfly effect coined by Edward Lorenz – small events having a major effect on seemingly unrelated major events at a later date. The butterfly effect was a metaphorical example of a tornado arising from the flapping of butterfly wings weeks earlier. It may be hard, if not impossible, to prove, especially when trying to link distant events to weather conditions, yet it's humbling to consider the conceptual importance of the butterfly effect in our lives. I propose that neutral is analogous to the butterfly effect in the sense of postulating delayed connections between apparently random happenings.

We use the term neutral for an event that does not cause an *observable* change; a car in neutral goes nowhere. I doubt that any neutral event is truly without consequence. A neutral mutation refers to an alteration in a gene that has no observable effect at the moment. However, that doesn't mean that the mutated gene, which produces a slightly altered protein, won't sooner or later in combination with other random changes have a biological effect. What is not observed – negative evidence – proves nothing. If you can't find your car keys, it doesn't mean they don't exist. My high school friend Van used to say that he never trusted himself when he said something was impossible or simply wrong, because he often awoke the next morning having changed his mind. Neutral events separated in time, like the butterfly effect, will almost certainly connect with something else in the future in an unexpected way. Give it time.

For example, how did you meet your spouse? Did you make an exhaustive survey of possible choices? Certainly not; that would be impossible. You might have gone by chance to a party or moved to a different city for a job. All happenstance, apparently neutral events, but not neutral at all; rather, disconnected events that converged at random at a later date. What appeared neutral changed your life (hopefully for the better!). I met my wife Lona on a blind date. She just happened to work at the National Institutes of Health, where I worked, and had a friend in common with me, not by choice, by happenstance, all neutral realties that all connected.

Love that butterfly! Fie on neutral, an erroneous concept! I'm reminded of the wise sign posted in the second-grade classroom of my son Anton: "Everything is something. Everything is connected to everything else. There's no such thing as a free lunch."

How about that for stretching the definition of neutral to include a silent label for happenings that become consequential in unexpected ways at some later time. Accept it: our destiny depends on the interaction of independent events, often considered neutral, leading to unintended results, leaving little room for the conceit of our brilliance and much space for gratitude.

Indifference

An early draft of my novel, *Jellyfish Have Eyes*, started with the discovery of a letter the protagonist, Ricardo, had written to his dead wife, Lillian, in which he bemoaned rotting in jail for the dubious felony of using taxpayers' funds to perform basic research on jellyfish that the conservative government considered irrelevant. Ricardo blamed the "Relevancers" – a faceless, abstract group I dreamed up – for his ill-fate. Ricardo writes in the letter, "At first, I did not believe that I was in serious trouble, but in retrospect I see that I had no chance. How did the Relevancers, whoever they are, gain such power? They talk of charity while they shoot to kill. Perhaps I'm too old and bitter to be objective. Did the Relevancers gain power with the approval, ignorance or indifference of society? Probably all three, although I fear indifference played the biggest role, probably the most dangerous situation."

Ricardo is a figment of my imagination, and no one today would be jailed for performing basic research on jellyfish. But Ricardo had a point about indifference, which he considered a powerful force fueled by silence, a silence Martin Luther King Jr. called appalling and equated to good people doing nothing about injustice. Both Ricardo and King extended the meaning of indifference to include not caring enough to act. How to persuade anyone of anything who doesn't care enough to act? I confess to having often straddled the fence by my inactions, essentially saying, "Perhaps I object, but not enough to put myself out, so maybe I concur."

Indifference or caring is a matter of degree and a question of how directly threatened or offended one feels. Take climate change, for instance. It's hard to imagine anyone truly disregarding the abundant evidence that climate change is a major threat to our way of life, indeed, to the planet, and yet it has an abstract quality, too distant to worry about for many people, more a far-off mirage than imminent reality. Too many care only to the point of indifference. And so, climate change is not resisted and will continue until it reaches the tipping point. Civilization suffers the consequences.

Oh, the malignancy of indifference, of not caring enough to act!

How harmless indifference looks, a bit like neutral! But don't be fooled: indifference defies combat while it attacks with invisible cannons. Indifference is a poor euphemism for not acting and for not confronting a shadow enemy. José Saramago's novel, *Seeing*, portrays the power of casting blank ballots in a political election: withdrawal, absence of action — a malign form of indifference — can carry a wallop, like silence, like neutral, all cousins under the umbrella of nothing.

Silence

When considering the power of silence, I wondered whether I could think of examples when less becomes more. Movies came to mind. One of my favorite Oscar-nominated movie categories is the short live pieces that range from approximately five to thirty minutes. These are analogous to short stories in literature. There's neither time for fluff nor irrelevant information. The heart of the story must be packaged in a condensed, clear form, like a swift punch in the gut.

In *Torsion* (2002), directed by Stefan Arsenijevic, a cow is ready to give birth in the midst of exploding bombs in war-torn Sarajevo. But the calf is locked in breech and threatens to kill the mother, a tragedy for both the cow, her calf and the farmer, whose livelihood depends on them. It's a tense scene. A choir on the way to Paris pauses on their trek to France to soothe the frantic cow by singing; mother calms down, and the calf is born. Art triumphs over war; humanity declares victory; birth and the continuity of life are celebrated, all in a few moments inspired by music. This masterful, antiwar short movie stunned me, and has had a lasting impact. We learn nothing about the farmer, the war, the members of the band, the back story or the future. All that is silent, as if it were non-existent, a silence that creates an unmistakable voice for on-going life despite the obstacles and hardships.

Another movie showed more directly the power of silence. *Sing*, a Hungarian film directed and written by Kristóf Deák, won the Oscar for short live movies at the 2017 Academy Awards ceremony. A young girl who loves to sing joins the choir but soon is told that she has no talent and must mime the words of the songs. She can stand with the others in the choir, but her voice must remain silent. It's a sham and a travesty. It turns out that other students were told the same thing. The teacher literally silenced the voices she deemed less gifted in order to not damage the chances of winning the interscholastic competition.

The girl, heartbroken, has a brainstorm: have everyone in the choir – everyone – mime the song at the competition! The choir appears on stage in front of a full house when the competition begins. The teacher-director starts to conduct, but she merely activates a choir of moving lips mouthing words that are not heard – no music, no sound – a protest of *silence*. The teacher is baffled, as is the audience. What a surrealistic scene! Moving lips and silence in a theater packed with confused spectators. The teacher laughs it off as, "What a cute joke. Okay, let's sing now." She raises the baton and tries again. Lips move, but still no voices are heard. She gets angry, and then angrier. The kids in the choir stick to their guns lacking bullets. Finally, the teacher stalks off, frustrated, defeated, humiliated. End of movie. There's no question about who won that battle. Silence defeated injustice This short film was as powerful as Ghandi's protests of peaceful resistance, the morality and message shouting louder than speech.

The silent movies of the early twentieth century also reveal benefits of limiting speech. At the Avalon Theater in Washington DC, I saw three silent movies – classics from the previous era – accompanied by music of the 1920s played by The

Peacherine Ragtime Society Orchestra. What an unexpected, thrilling evening! I saw *Habeus Corpus* (1928) starring Stan Laurel and Oliver Hardy, *The Adventurer* (1917) starring a very young Charlie Chaplin, and *One Week* (1920) starring Buster Keaton, all with subtitles.

An enthusiastic audience of old-timers (like Lona and me!) as well as younger folks filled the theater with sporadic loud clapping, holding their hands high above their heads to emphasize their appreciation. I laughed out loud, especially during the Laurel and Hardy movie. I can think of no greater comedy team in the history of movies than these two geniuses. The absence of voices revealed how their skillful timing enhanced interactions and their ability to project both humor and pathos, how two complementary personalities blended to make one creative, silent individual. The astounding ability of these brilliant actors to convey conflicts was so much more effective than the bombastic scenes of the popular blockbusters of today, which pummel our ears with noise-invading decibels.

Sharp movements, small gestures and facial expressions of these early movie actors, artists of their times, projected their feelings couched in slapstick. When Charlie Chaplin was being chased by the police while he was courting a young lady in *The Adventurer*, I felt genuinely sad when she turned away from him after discovering he was an escaped convict. Chaplin showed his crushed feeling by only small changes in his body language lasting seconds. Less gave so much more; not a word spoken.

Watching these movies brought large expanses of time together for me. I remember when I was a toddler watching Laurel and Hardy on television with my mother. We were laughing until an abrupt switch to a sad scene of some sort, never mind exactly what that scene was. What did count, what I remember, was the tears I saw in my mother's eyes. "You're crying," I said, as she wiped her face self-consciously. Like I said, they were geniuses of projecting the human soul without fanfare, from laughter to tears and back again, with focus on individuals and common experiences rather than on today's three E's, as I call them: Extravagances and Explosions Everywhere.

These silent movies accompanied by the ragtime accompaniment of the Scott Joplin era also made me think of my father in Russia circa 1910 playing the cello in the orchestra pits of silent movies as a young boy not even 10 years old. His father – my grandfather – had abandoned his home in Moscow by going to St. Petersburg for months to improve as an amateur violinist, leaving my father, not even a teenager but already a gifted cellist, to support his mother and three siblings. Thus, I felt a personal connection between him and these silent movies, accompanied by music, as I watched these treasures on screen

How would I have reacted to these silent movies if the extensive changes I have lived through hadn't occurred? What appears old fashioned today because of technology and myriad other changes can easily be misjudged as simplistic. These masters were artists, reminding me that the beginning stages of any new endeavor, such as these movies, are far from primitive. In the uncertain future, our views of today will no doubt appear old fashioned to future generations. Remembering the past, respecting it, recognizing how much it has to offer may serve us well as time moves on.

Two more silences come to mind, both nature's dispassionate, mysterious children. One is threatening, sometimes deadly, the other extraordinary. The dangerous silence is that of illness that strikes without warning: cancer, diabetes, some viruses. Covid-19 runs amok throughout the world as I write sheltered at home, hiding from this quiet, tiny beast that lurks silently wherever I go and whatever I touch. Where did this virus come from, how long will it last, how do we protect ourselves from this silent, invisible enemy? How to kill what doesn't breathe?

The other silence few have witnessed, but I have been fortunate enough to encounter as a scientist: the silence of nature's mysteries. I'm reminded of when my colleague Joe and I waited one night for several hours on a dock in La Parguera, Puerto Rico, for jellyfish to be attracted to a light. The evening was still and silent, and it seemed that no jellyfish would answer our luminous call. After three hours or so, as if by magic, five jellyfish, each following one another as if on parade, pulsed slowly upward to the surface from the depth, their long trailing tentacles reflecting the light that we cast upon the water. They approached us with the silent majesty of royalty, bringing with them many questions. Where were they earlier? What took them so long to appear? Why did they come at all? How do they perceive light with their ancient eyes? What did they hope to find, if anything? Are they ever satisfied or disappointed? What motivates jellyfish, which have inhabited Earth for seven to eight hundred million years? Were the jellyfish at all aware of where they were going? Oh, there's so much more to nature's silent mysteries: how do genes function, how do strands of DNA make babies? What fills the space between galaxies and where does the universe end, if it does? These miracles are the great silences of the unknown.

Numbers

Here's irony worthy of thought: there's truth in numbers. Really? Maybe. We consider numbers objective – 8 is 8, not 7 or 9 – an expression of reality for making life seem absolute by quantitative truths. But numbers are abstract and relative, like so much in our lives. We can't touch or visualize or assign a color to a number. A number, any number, is neither large nor small: it's a relative size. One day is an eternity for a young child to wait for a present, while one second contains more lifetimes than I can imagine for some elementary particles. Yet, we say, "I'll be there in a second." When is that?

Am I speaking in riddles, accelerating to get nowhere? Perhaps. The doctor asks you to rate your pain between 1 and 10. How ridiculous to pinpoint pain with a number, which is subjectively different for each person.

I recently visited Biltmore, the formidable estate of George Vanderbilt in Asheville, North Carolina. To say it is a grand estate, large and magnificent, makes little impression. Abstractions seldom do. But to say the estate is on 8000 acres (originally 125,000 acres) and the mansion has 250 rooms – now you get a feel for the place. The image is getting framed; the numerical limits define the abstract description. For landscaping,

Vanderbilt planted 3 million trees. That's a forest, no longer a garden, and the number makes that distinction clear.

Numbers impress: I visited the botanical gardens in Asheville (separate from the Vanderbilt estate) where they have scattered animals made from Lego. One was a butterfly. It was beautiful, but what impressed me was that it was made from 60,549 pieces of Lego!

There may be relatively little difference in skill between football or baseball teams, but we are in awe of the number one team, the winner on top of the ladder. But what if the same teams played each other without generating a hierarchy, winners and losers, the champion and everyone else. There would be no structure, and I believe, we would lose interest. Exhibition games are not exciting. If the score doesn't matter who cares? Even in art – a non-competitive activity or one that should be – a hierarchy of value exists by the price paid for the piece. Auctions are exciting because of the amount of money someone is willing to pay for an object while the object itself often has limited interest in comparison.

It's all about abstract numbers bending and framing and creating an objective reality from a subjective world. Without numbers, which have no intrinsic value, we would be living different lives with different values and different goals and, perhaps, different concepts of happiness and who we are.

Erewhon

The novel *Erewhon* by Samuel Butler, a satire on Victorian society, first published anonymously in 1872, introduces us to a foreign lifestyle. I was. already intrigued by the title: the name of a fictional country meaning "nowhere" spelled backwards with the letters "h" and "w" transposed.

The laws in Erewhon are bizarrely different from those in our culture. Because in Erewhonian society, unlike in our society, individuals who commit crimes – forgery, burglary, assault – are considered to be "suffering from a severe fit of immorality." Instead of jail, those convicted are hospitalized, treated and returned to society. Specialized "straighteners," individuals "who bendeth back the crooked" can return them the right path, and all is forgiven.

Erewhonians with any illness, however, are considered criminal and are imprisoned. Equally incredible is that "poverty and ill luck are also considered criminal." In brief, Erewhonians are punished for their misfortune. Physicians practice secretly and can be consulted only at great risk. In one trial in Erewhon, the lawyer tried to defend a young man coughing and accused of having consumption by saying he was faking it for insurance money, which would have been only immoral, not criminal, and curable by hospitalization. The defense didn't work, the patient was convicted of illness and given a life sentence in jail. The poor victim accepted the sentence, saying he thought he was given a fair trial.

Wow!

Erewhon is fiction, of course, a satire in a setting of a country situated "nowhere," where the laws are totally foreign to our viewpoint. But then, I thought, instead of "nowhere," *Erewhon* could read "here now" by a slight rearrangement of the letters, and that brought to mind a pet peeve of mine. Why do we often blame ourselves – feel guilty – about our health issues when we have done nothing wrong?

Is there a sliver of *Erewhon* culture lurking in our own? For example, I have an incurable sweet tooth. Candy bars, chocolate in all forms, desserts – I love them all! I've often wanted to start with dessert as an appetizer before I tackle an entrée. I've never done that, coward that I seem to be.

At a restaurant I choose carefully, doing my best to limit calories and fat in a course that my palate will accept. Though I've eaten enough chicken that I fear sprouting feathers, fish are only tolerable (halibut is my favorite since it doesn't have much taste), but I'll never grow scales. I've adhered to the saying that the best fish doesn't taste like fish! Hardly a strong endorsement.

It turns out I'm not the only one counting calories and trying (not always successfully) to eat with good health in mind, to practice selective deprivation. Nothing wrong about that, but what about that nagging feeling of guilt that poisons our enjoyment, that internal voice saying, "I should know better!" Here's an example. The other evening with friends at a restaurant, a first for all of us, the conversation went something like this:

"What a find! Great food!"

"Agreed. I'd come here again in a heartbeat."

Then the waiter arrived. "Anyone for dessert? Shall I bring a menu?"

We all sheepishly feigned being stuffed; we couldn't force down another mouthful.

"No thanks," said one of the guests.

Others nodded.

As usual, I was the loose cannon. "Well, are you all sure? Maybe we should just see what they have. That doesn't mean we need to order it."

"Oh, okay," said another.

I sensed a crack in the armor.

We scrutinized the menu and discussed how sinful (note the guilt) the desserts were – chocolate, sugar, cream – terrible, irresponsible...delicious. We ordered one dessert for the table that seemed not too fattening (naturally, not my first choice) and we all had just enough to whet our appetite for more, complaining that we had eaten too much and feeling...yes, you guessed it...GUILTY! We'd trespassed the doctor's orders and our line of obedience.

I agree that we should eat reasonably and take responsibility for our health. That's not the issue here. I'm considering the bigger picture of how we view the human condition. It seems that we often feel personally at fault for health issues. If we're overweight, we lack self-control, ignoring metabolic differences among people or circumstances that come and go; if we get the flu, we haven't washed our hands enough or kept clear of crowds during flu season, or we've rubbed shoulders with someone coughing when we should have kept our distance; if we get winded when climbing stairs, we haven't exercised sufficiently. Shame on us. Sometimes it's more serious, like blaming ourselves for a heart attack because we didn't go right away to a cardiologist when we had a few sporadic, ambiguous symptoms, nothing alarming. Ditto for cancer, our fault for a delayed check-up, too busy to see the doctor.

I'm not advocating a cavalier attitude toward our health. Goodness no! Adherence to modern medicine has brought prolonged health – sixties are the new fifties – and increased longevity. But where's the line we cross that puts us at fault for much of life's toll on us, or just able to enjoy the moment – yes, "sin" – with a molten chocolate dessert? Can't we be responsible without being under a blanket of guilt for not obsessing enough about ourselves? Is it always our "fault" if we get sick or gain a few pounds and develop a less than perfect physique (which we hopefully reverse!) or show signs of aging?

Why can't we rejoice for our good health when we have it and enjoy it guilt-free and still be responsible?]We're not Erewhonians, thank goodness! Let's keep that country "nowhere" rather than "here now."

Evolvability

To what extent does the future govern our lives? Let's say I was guaranteed (impossible, of course) that I would live an extended life, but was also assured that planet Earth would be destroyed soon after my death, perhaps by a collision with a giant meteor, or maybe a plague would wipe life or perhaps only people off the planet. Would I continue as usual if I knew there wouldn't be a future for those left behind? Is this an absurd question? I don't think so. The question is couched in evolvability, an esoteric concept derived by biologists interested in evolution. Evolvability is a fascinating scientific question that I relate here to our own lives. Please bear with me for a little science.

First, I'll tell you what evolvability isn't: it's not a visible part of evolution, such as fossils. It's an invisible concept. Evolution (which incredibly some skeptics still deny) depends on random genetic mutations, most of which are harmful and die out over time. In rare instances, a mutation causes a beneficial change that gives the organism an advantage and makes it more "fit" to survive and reproduce than its peers. These rare, good mutations are passed on to the progeny, which ultimately, boosted by accumulation of more mutations, changing environmental conditions and new niches, lead to the evolution of new species. Such is biological evolution: selecting for new traits popping up at random that make the organism able to cope and reproduce more successfully than its fellow species under existing – *present* – conditions. Present conditions, that's the key here.

Enter the concept of evolvability, which is selection for the *ability* to adapt, not selection for the adaptive change itself. You may wonder, as many scientists do, how can the ability to succeed in the future drive what happens now? The future is an assumption that never arrives; it's abstract, without "teeth," as it were. While the past provides the foundation and the present challenges survival, what role, if any, might the imaginary future, a silent period that is always present yet never here, play in evolution?

There is no conclusive answer to this teasing question about the future. Evolvability is thought-provoking, however, because of the inevitability of constantly changing conditions, which makes species tread in treacherous waters to stay afloat. Only an adaptive creature, an organism that is sufficiently robust to withstand hardships and make changes quickly, can survive when conditions change, which would make the *ability* to adapt readily, an important trait enabling the organism to continue evolution's journey.

In brief, the future requires species to be adaptive in order to survive. If evolvability exists at all – if the future has a role in evolution by selecting for adaptability – it ensures our proteins do their job efficiently, but not so efficiently that there isn't "wiggle room." They are not so perfectly sculpted for their present function that they can't easily change or expand their functions. In other words, the "wiggle room" gives proteins the potential to perform more than one function. Proteins must be practical beasts and able to switch roles for expediency, to remain flexible, robust and able to cope with unexpected changes. Without a future, of course, there would be no need for flexibility, since there would be no evolution.

And what about the fidelity of our genes? Do they remain absolutely identical when they replicate No. If genes didn't make accidental mistakes, that is, if they didn't mutate occasionally (very rarely) at random, they wouldn't have the resources that allow their host to cope when conditions change, which conditions always do. Without accidental mutations evolution wouldn't exist; that genes are prone to making errors becomes the artillery to conquer the new obstacles that appear in the future.

Pretty amazing thought, no? Mistakes allow us to stay alive. The future, which never arrives, affects the present, which is always here. I was impressed by the merging of the present with the future when I watched the Sailor Circus with my grandkids in Sarasota. In the circus, all the performers were children, yet they acted as mature, accomplished adults: they were living in two time zones simultaneously, the present and the future. Which brings me back to the beginning of this essay. How many of our present decisions are made on the basis of planning for our abstract future? Also, to what extent do we prepare to leave a footprint, a legacy, in a future we will never see or know? In a phrase, to what extent do we live in imaginary future time?

I believe we inhabit the future in more ways than we realize. Therefore, I assume the world will live-on beyond me and I continue to think that my contributions – grandchildren, science findings, even this essay – will extend to and make that abstract future a reality. Would I continue to lead my life as I do if I knew the future for everyone would disappear with me?

I don't know.

SCIENCE AND WRITING

Cracks

My urge to write in earnest started when I was 56 on vacation in Maine, and fully engaged in my career in science. I wrote a three-page story about an American teenage boy visiting the Arctic. The boy went hunting with an Inuit boy of the same age, and they killed a caribou. The narrative described the majesty of the barren tundra glittering with reflected sunshine, while the narrator, the visitor – my alter ego – dwelled on thoughts of life and death as the caribou's blood soaked into the white snow. I loved creating a foreign universe on paper populated by my thoughts and dreams. I wanted to continue writing after I returned from my vacation, but my obligations as a scientist limited my time. What to do? I decided to write in sporadic, short intervals – an hour or two here and there on weekends or evenings – and not worry about finishing anything. I would write without a goal and accumulate thoughts that might form a foundation for future writing, if and when my time allowed it. I thought of those brief, random periods for writing as cracks of time, which got me thinking about cracks in general, and led to the essay, excerpted here.

Cracks have developed a bad reputation and are considered blemishes. Cracked implies broken, ready to be discarded.

"He's a crackpot! What's he thinking – that he can part the Red Sea? That he's Moses?" Such a crackpot needs to be avoided. We commonly believe that the crack damages the object, the bone, the appearance, the value. We tend to think of cracks as a liability, a sign of deterioration. How limited a view, how shallow!

Imagine this: the dinner guests are coming in an hour. What to do? Spruce up the place, read a few pages of that interminable novel, flip on the TV? How many times have you had this dilemma? There's not enough time to accomplish much, but too much time to waste counting molecules of air. Lost time? That depends.

Consider the 60 minutes a precious gift. I did that once some time ago. It went like this: it was 5 o'clock and I wondered what to do before the guests arrived at six. Write perhaps? I started scribbling thoughts, never mind how good or bad they were, and put them in this crack of time.

Are you obsessed by monoliths, those huge things we lump as one, like career, success, failure, what we believe to be important in life? And important they are. But look more closely. These are riddled with cracks in the form of interruptions and setbacks. The bulk is bits pieced together to make a single image, like a puzzle. And what is between those pieces? Cracks, of course.

There are maturing cracks that evolve graciously with time, such as cracks of paint on an old master portrait – a Vermeer or Rembrandt. Not planned, not wanted, yet beautiful marks of age and authenticity. Like the deep creases that line an old friend's forehead earned by weathering the storm and navigating obstacles. Yet people reach for that miracle drug Botox to eliminate those distinctive cracks. And the result: a smooth, blank, expressionless stare. What a shame. And then there are those soft wrinkles extending from smiling eyes which draw you in and give you comfort. Those are cracks as well – creases that whisper kindness and understanding.

Cracks give entry points, such as a lover's note slipped through the crack beneath the bedroom door or wedged along the side. A crack in armor can bring down tyrants. A wisecrack can devastate or save the day – it all depends on timing and intent.

And what about solid cracks in empty space? The fine strands of a spider's cobweb are nothing more than cracks in the continuity of air, firm cracks of fine silk that sustain the spider. Then there's the painted streak that divides the road in equal halves and leaves a precious crack of space to prevent the crack of colliding cars shouting death before its time.

Nature cracks with power. There's the piercing crack of thunder that precedes the jagged cracks of lightning, instants that enliven and alarm. There are the devastating popping cracks of burning wood in raging forest fires, but there's also the comforting cracks in the fireplace with multicolored flames.

Beware the frightening crack of avalanches when skiing in the silence of a snowy mountain, or the crack of breaking ice when kayaking in an Arctic bay beneath a glacier calving its mighty iceberg progeny.

There is the crack of authority: a bullwhip's snap or a gavel's pound.

How sweet the cracking sounds of victory: the crack when the swinging bat contacts the baseball, or the crack that drives the golf ball towards the pin, or the crack of the well-timed tennis serve that scores an ace and wins the point.

There's the "breakthrough" crack. "If only I could crack it..." To penetrate the barrier of ignorance means advancement, hope and glory.

Most complex of all are the imagined cracks you cannot see or hear, the ones that mark the lines that must not be crossed. Those invisible, elusive cracks drawn by parents, boss or lover keep us on the beaten path or sculpt our lives into contorted shapes.

Put aside your prejudice against the maligned cracks, for they punctuate our lives.

Publishing

Publishing glitters as an end point for the research projects of a scientist. In my 50 years of science, I published numerous articles in professional journals, chapters in textbooks and reference books, and a book, *Gene Sharing and Evolution,* extending my research on gene expression in the eye. Publishing science, always challenging, requires valid experiments, clear presentation, proper referencing to previous studies, and verifiable conclusions. My science publications became their own reward, with each a stepping-stone for progress. But then what, after publication? My focus switched to the next science project. Apart from presentations at scientific meetings and academic institutions, I depended on a professional audience to find my publications. I let the chips fall where they may; that's the publishing life for a scientist, at least it was for me.

I realized when I closed my research laboratory to devote my time to writing of a very different sort — novels, essays, memoir — that publishing would be very challenging at best. I did not anticipate, however, the extent to which I would need to be involved in generating a market and promoting a published book. Writing and selling were inseparable, and I was naïve.

I was often asked, "Are you writing for your family?"

"Well, I hope they read what I write, but no, I'm writing for anyone and everyone who will read my stuff," I said. What author doesn't want his or her book read, at least by a few people other than immediate family and friends?

My friends and colleagues smiled, politely, a quiet way of saying, "Really? You're a scientist. It's hard out there for a novice writer, an old one at that."

Or, was I hearing my private fear of giving up science and embarking as a writer at 69?

Advance past the years taking workshops in fiction, past the long hours and days and months of writing and rewriting short stories that were rejected by literary journals with no helpful explanation, past the many drafts (28 revisions of one sort or another!) of my novel, *Jellyfish Have Eyes*, and past having an agent for a year who finally bowed out, admitting defeat. I queried 128 other agents for my novel; only 19 replied. One wanted to see 50 pages and then, in so many words, said, "No dice," providing comments that were mostly incorrect due, I believe, to rapid skimming.

More frustration. Small presses usually take months to reply, and apparently less than 1% (a soft number that must vary with the press) of submitted books are published.

Scientists are pampered by comparison. Response to submitted manuscripts to scientific journals are received typically within a few weeks. Sometimes the article is rejected outright because the manuscript is not well suited for that journal. Disappointing, but relatively little time has elapsed and there are numerous other journals to try again. And again. Peers review the submitted manuscripts and their comments – favorable or critical – are sent to the author. What luxury: free feedback! The scientist now has guidance for revision of the rejected manuscript, which is often reconsidered by the journal. If not, the comments are helpful for submission to another journal, and there are many. Most articles eventually find a publisher in a scientific journal.

But non-science is different. Fiction can be self-published, which is not a realistic option in science. I considered that possibility for my novel after attending a self-publishing symposium at The Writer's Center in Bethesda. I didn't want the novel to die quietly in my desk drawer. Now, the turning point. I was in the waiting room for an appointment with the editor of a recommended self-publishing house in New York, when my cell phone rang.

"I'm calling from IPBooks. We want to publish your novel."

Could this be true, or was I actually watching a movie with a last-minute rescue from some horrible fate? IPBooks, an independent publisher that my friend Carolyn Feigelson had recommended, stood for International Psychoanalytic Books. Since my novel had nothing to do with psychology and nine months had passed since I submitted the manuscript, I had given up on them. But suddenly, with timing as serendipitous as if in a movie, they accepted my novel! I rationalized that introspective Ricardo, the protagonist, appealed to the publisher. In any case, IPBooks was a legitimate publisher based in New York. Hooray! I went directly to speak to them.

"My wife loved your novel, and she is a hard critic," said Arnold Richards, the publisher. Thank goodness for kind spouses! I didn't bother to ask whether he too liked the novel but assumed he did. After some editing, the novel was published (*Jellyfish Have Eyes*; 2014), and I was thrust into the quagmire of marketing. Readers don't grow on trees, and as a scientist and non-entity as a writer, I was overwhelmed by how to market the book. I found myself in two conflicting worlds: an author struggling to write, and a prospective salesman, not knowing how to market. And, I had qualms about shouting, "Look what I've written! Come one, come all! Wonderful novel for sale!"

I was told that I needed to develop a following on social media to attract potential readers. "People buy brands, the authors, as much as the book itself," said those in the know. Science certainly hadn't prepared me for this. Moreover, I'm no computer nerd, the hub of social media. Computer technology was a struggle for me in science as well. Add to that the uncertainty of how much to reveal about myself. Confusing for a twentieth century man in the twenty-first century. I felt old trying to act young. I didn't want to cling to the past and needed to return to grade school. Too late for that. I was recycling myself, excited in my fatigue, challenged to do "it" all over again, without being able to define "it."

Another challenge to conquer as a novice author was book fairs. My friend Neal Gillen invited me to participate in the annual University Club book fair in Washington D.C. I remember sitting with stacks of my novel carefully arranged on a table, my pen ready for signing the dozens of copies I planned to sell. Oh, the pride of authorship! Strangers walked by. Some noticed me, others pretended not to, a few glanced at my book, very occasionally someone picked it up to read the blurbs on the back, and then replaced it, sometimes with a polite smile. Get used to it, I told myself, preparing to embrace my new world. I was a writer now, wasn't I? An hour went by. The crowd was increasing and milling around. Not a book sold by me. Finally, a man picked up my novel and paged through it. I stood up and gave my spiel, feeling clumsy. He nodded. "Interesting," he said. How would he know? I doubt he even knew what a jellyfish was. He put the book back on the table. I sat down again, disheartened.

I was a failure.

An author across the way trapped potential buyers like a cowboy with a lasso. "Hello, there," he said to someone walking by, not noticing him in the same fashion that he hadn't noticed me a moment earlier. "It's many short stories you can read whenever you have a few moments. Keep it by your bedside," barks the genius author/salesman. The man comes closer, picks up the book. "It's only $12, a bargain. I'll sign it for you now," he continued. Yes, that's right. The man bought the book, and many others did too.

I felt like shit.

I wasn't so gifted. There were others like me who sat behind their tables like part of the furniture. Poor souls. Poor me. I bought a book from the author of a neighboring table that I had little intention of reading because I felt sorry for him; no one had even looked in his direction. I did sell a few books. Two? Three? Hard to keep track. I wondered who would actually read it.

Then there was the Kensington book fair a few months later. Again, I sat behind my table, my books stacked artfully. Again, strangers walked by. But I hoped I was getting better. I greeted them more effectively, understood more what it's all about: reaching people, like it was when presenting a poster at a scientific meeting. It's the person, the scientist or author, that needs to make it interesting at first. It's not easy, but I sold a few books. But then there was the man who walked by with his young son on his shoulders. The father was staring straight ahead, robot-like, but his son, bless his young curiosity, saw my sign with a picture of a jellyfish. "Hey, look!" he exclaimed. "Jellyfish!!" How I loved that kid. But his father, unimpressed, didn't flinch and kept walking. Oh, well...Another kid came along with Mom. He was about 10 or so, if that, and picked up the book, looking serious.

"Very interesting," he said, like a professor.

"Thanks," I responded.

"These are box jellyfish, are they not?"

Was he for real? "Yes," I answered, as if I talked to all 10-year-odd kids about science and philosophy.

"Just where are the eyes?" he asked.

By now I accepted him as an educated adult, maybe even a precocious professor after all. "Well," I said, "this species (and I threw in the species name, *Tripedalia cystophora*, for good measure) has four specialized organs surrounding its surface called rhopalia (another scientific gem he needed to know) that contain the eyes." I could have provided more information, but really...he was 10 years old.

"Oh, I see," he said. His mother told him they should move along. "Thanks," said the boy, and he put the book back on the table.

"Is he learning all this at school?" I asked his mother.

"No. He reads. He knows everything."

Oh, yeah. He didn't know what my book's about. He should have bought one to read in his spare time, and maybe another for a sister he might have had.

After a while, I realized how silly for me to sell these books. I'm unknown as a writer, jellyfish aren't exactly the hot topic of the times, and I needed people to read the novel, not pay me a few dollars. Why didn't I just give books to people stopping by and hesitating? That made sense to me. I gave away two books and was starting to feel more comfortable, less self-conscious. A new world was opening before my eyes and I was experimenting how to navigate those turbulent waters, how to take chances and how to live in the two conflicting worlds: writing and selling, doing and managing, creating and surviving. No activity is just one thing. Think of this essay. It's writing about selling!

Time went by and I've been fortunate in having Stevan Nikolic, the founder and editor or Adelaide Books (New York and Lisbon) publish my memoir, *The Speed of Dark*, which has opened the literary door to publishing for me. When I went to the Frankfurt Book Fair, Adelaide Books displayed my memoir in grand style. *The Speed of Dark* lined the top two rows of shelves of the booth and an impressive poster promoting my book towered over me. This larger than life-size poster consisted of the cover image of the memoir, my name and the title given in ten languages. What a wonderful step-up into the world stage of publishing for a research scientist turned author!

Another equally tall poster about Adelaide Books stood beside the one promoting my book. The middle of the poster stated:

We Don't Publish

Classics

We Make

Classics

Oh yes, a concise statement reflecting my own inclinations. No, not that my memoir is a classic. The inclination not to follow the masses; rather, breathe life into obscurity, discover hidden treasures, esoteric possibilities, new ideas and neglected corners. Experiment until it works. This was my goal as a scientist when I studied the little-known eye lens of scallops and jellyfish, which few even knew had eyes. I hoped to continue in that vein as a writer.

Many fascinating books caught my eye as I toured the booths of traditional and independent publishers at the Frankfurt Book Fair. Although the large commercial publishers presented a potpourri of wonderful books (if only I had time to read more of them), many were by or about celebrities or about hot topics of the times. By contrast, I was impressed with the diversity of books at the independent publishers, which suggested a freedom and curiosity reminiscent of my life as a research scientist probing new areas. My publisher, Adelaide Books, published poetry, essays, short stories, and novels, written by authors expressing and testing themselves, some young, others older. The boundaries were porous; the focus was quality. I sensed a love for writing rather than a quest for sales. I was happy to have my memoir included.

On the last day of the Book Fair, I signed copies of my memoir for interested readers. Shortly afterwards, when I was on my way out, one of the women came running up to me.

"Oh, I'm glad I caught you before you left," she said. "I want to thank you so much for the memoir."

Flattered, I replied, "It's I who thanks you for your interest." What a welcome difference from my earlier frustrations at book fairs.

"I paged through the book quickly and saw you're a molecular biologist. So am I!"

She had done research on immunology. I suddenly realized the importance of writing who I am. I knew this, of course, but to see its rewards in a stranger in a foreign country in the midst of so many books by distinguished and striving authors drove the point home of being authentic.

Publishing meant accepting myself. Immersion with international publishers in Frankfurt, with the support of Adelaide Books, made this experience a lasting memory.

Truth and Fantasy

As a scientist, I concerned myself with truth, defined by what I could verify either by referring to what others had shown, what I had experienced myself, or what I could support with my experimental data. Even then, the experimental results needed confirmation by repetition and, ultimately, by other laboratories. Yet, even if a scientific discovery is correct – true – and supported by solid data, it can be rejected or ignored unless connected to an accepted structure of knowledge, which is known as the 'principle of correspondence'. The brilliant 1865 experiments on pea plants by the Augustinian friar and scientist, Johann Gregor Mendel, that lay down the foundation of genetics is a prime example. Mendel's correct laws of inheritance were ignored until rediscovered in 1900 when science had advanced. To be accepted and acknowledged, truth in science requires a verifiable construct.

Science, however, is not a basketful of facts about nature. The facts – data – must be linked in a narrative that supports, advances, modifies or upsets current interpretations or theories. Such linkage aims to fill the cracks of ignorance between the facts.

As an aside, imaginative narratives also have a history of foreshadowing scientific truths. Jonah Lehrer points out in a series of remarkable essays, *Proust is a Neuroscientist*, how diverse artists – painters, composers, writers, even a chef – have foreshadowed scientific truths. Such foreshadowing has occurred many times. A well-known example is *2001: A Space Odyssey*, Stanley Kubrick's 1968 classic movie that predicts the computer age.

Writing, as science, also requires adherence to truth. When I wrote my memoir, I certainly couldn't escape facts; it would be unacceptable to describe events I never experienced or to be influenced by fictitious people. Truth in memoir, however, is less rigorous than that in science. Memoir relies on memory, which blurs and gets modified with time. Also, past experiences cannot be repeated or verified as scientific experiments. Truth in memoir has no predictive value, as it has in science.

When I wrote short stories – fiction – truth slipped another notch. I created imaginary characters and put them in made up situations. At first, I believed truth in fiction was whatever I said it was, but it turned out that was not strictly correct. I was surprised when I workshopped one of my first short stories and heard, "That's impossible, it's too coincidental." But I asked, what if a similar situation actually did occur? No dice. That didn't solve the problem. The instructor, Robert Bausch, explained that in real life every event had an explanation, whether or not the cause was known, while in fiction that wasn't true; the events had to be earned, embedded somehow in the story to be accepted. Even fiction, then, had to have some consistency with reality in the story to be credible.

But what about fantasy, ideas that float into areas we have never experienced or that even contradict what we have experienced? Would that allow the creation of a new reality that had nothing to do with the reality we know? How firm are the boundaries that define our reality? For example, although physicians have debated pinpointing exactly when death in humans takes place – when there is no more pulse or brain waves – everyone agrees that dead and alive are mutually incompatible states. Being both dead and alive at the same time is fantasy, not within our concept of reality. Life and death are defined by being separate. Death wouldn't exist without life, and life would need redefinition without death.

In my short story collection, *Notes Going Underground*, I explored the overlapping states of life and death. In one story, a dead man gives his own eulogy at his funeral service as his remaining life passes slowly into his corpse in a coffin by his side. In another story, a man, pronounced dead by a doctor, remains alive as his life seeps away slowly. He attends his own funeral service and says goodbye during his burial.

When I mentioned these fantasy stories to a friend, she shook her head and said, "I have no interest in such nonsense. I don't like fantasy or the supernatural."

This response reminded me of the earlier criticism of my short story in which fiction was not accepted because the sequence of events was too coincidental. Did fantasy also need to cling to an accepted structure of reality? I wondered how other authors dealt with this. I thought of Mary Shelley's classic fantasy, *Frankenstein*, in which Frankenstein used spare parts of a corpse to create a living monster – life from death. While this fantasy crosses the thick boundary between life and death, the monster is still portrayed with emotions that we can understand. For example, he is miserable for not being loved and excluded from his society. Thus, the monster is not alive in the conventional way of being born like us, he is still underlined by a humanity we have experienced. The fantasy keeps a foothold on our concept of reality.

There's the classic fantasy of Franz Kafka's *Metamorphosis*, a transition from man to insect that took place even before the story begins. Yet, it's not the idea that the story's protagonist, Gregor, transitioned from man to insect that makes the story powerful. Gregor the insect continues to think, suffer and struggle as the human being he was before the transition, since he is a Janus figure. In Roman mythology, Janus is revered as the god of transitions with two faces – one facing forward (in Gregor's case, his fate as an insect) – and the other backward (his life as a human). The supernatural transformation submits to the reality of human suffering that can be imagined and experienced.

These fantasy transitions are accepted because they are solidly implanted in the real world of our experience. Crossing the border separating life and death is also within my concept of reality in my short stories. The man giving his own eulogy at his funeral as well as the man attending his own funeral after a physician declared him dead are fantasies, but the core of the stories is about explorations of identity in living terms that pertain to our common experiences. Whether doing scientific research or experimentation or writing fiction and fantasy, I never escape the need for truth, as I experience it.

Opening Doors

When I started writing fiction each thought prompted the next by linking ideas as they came to me. I did not design my stories, but let ideas and images become open doors to enter. For example, in *Little Boy Juan*, the nine-year-old boy was banned to an empty room by his teacher for talking in class. She told him to think about keeping quiet while exiled alone. Many thoughts, one leading to another, went through Juan's mind, and these became a portrait of how Juan as he saw the world:

"Think about keeping quiet," kept echoing in Juan's mind, but he kept running into the problem that, as far as he was concerned, thinking was a type of talking, and that wasn't quiet. He tried to think so silently that no one would be able to hear it. That didn't work. Thinking was thinking. If he had to stop thinking altogether to learn new things in class, as Ms Sprinkle said, he would never learn anything.

"I'm just dumb," he told himself, but he didn't really believe it."

Juan's thoughts ran freely as he remained banished in the empty classroom:

"The sun peeked out from behind the cloud for a moment and shined directly in Juan's eyes, then disappeared again behind a black cloud, returning the room to a drab, unfriendly gray. Juan saw streaks of water flowing down the window. "I knew it smelled like rain," he said to himself, and this was comforting. He always loved rain for some reason. He didn't have to go outside at recess in the rain, and in Puerto Rico they even closed the schools if it rained hard enough. He liked the idea of recess, but the reality was that he always stood around by himself while everyone else seemed to be having so much fun together. He didn't mind so much being alone, but it was embarrassing, like holding a sign saying, 'no one likes me'."

When I presented this story in a fiction workshop, I was surprised how many people thought that it needed a plot beyond steam of consciousness and introspection, it needed something at stake. In order to comply and provide a worrisome consequence for Juan's misbehavior, I added his fear that his mother would punish him for talking in class by cancelling a scheduled playdate for Saturday with Katie, a girl he liked in his class.

I understand the power of conflict and setting up obstacles and consequences in stories. But I question the necessity of always adding something at stake to keep the reader turning pages. Aren't internal ruminations that go through a little's boy mind when he's punished enough for an interesting story? Several children about Juan's age told me they identified with him in the story. They didn't need further conflict. I explored Juan as I would study nature as a scientist, step-by-step, revealing rather than imposing. What could be more compelling than the human mind? I considered my challenge as a writer, then, as much to inhabit the characters, fictional or real, to explore the complexity of their minds as to place artificial obstacles in their path. Does a writer always need to add intrigue and exterior conflict to create a compelling story?

For example, the Belgium-French movie, *The Unknown Girl*, kept my attention from the outset, although nothing was at stake. A doctor who lived for her work and to help others did not answer a doorbell late at night after her office was closed. The next day a young unidentified African immigrant girl was found dead nearby. The security camera showed that she was the woman who rang the doorbell. Out of guilt for not responding to the doorbell, the doctor went on an all-out search for the woman's identity so that she would not be lost to the world. Discovering the dead woman's identity was driven by curiosity, not a consequence. The search exposed the nature of the doctor and the fate of the unfortunate victim, a teenage prostitute, and how she affected a few people in her short life. Complicating the plot with conflicts or consequences for not being able to identify her would have made a different movie, perhaps in some respects more fashionable or compelling, but I doubt it would have made it better.

Juan thought about what he found intriguing as a boy – his questions and speculations were his doors to open. The unknown prostitute in the movie may have died because a young doctor didn't open a door to her office one night. We'll never know. The doors we open are what the stories are about. Leaving doors open help readers enter their own stories rather than the author's. That has happened to me both as a reader and a writer. For example, I have a weakness for Don Quixote, not because of his charging windmills in a suit of armor among his many creative adventures, but because through his story I imagine my own dreams of triumph and pursue my own eccentric thoughts. As a writer, I was surprised by a comment from a scientist in his seventies that my novel, *Jellyfish Have*

Eyes, showed that Ricardo, a scientist in his seventies, should have called it quits, retired, and know better than to keep working, a point of view that never crossed my mind when I was writing the book. In another comment, a reader who spent his life as a business executive told me that the guilty person in my novel was the Scientific Director – the boss – who allowed the protagonist to act as he did, another interpretation that I never intended. Fiction becomes malleable and personal when it invades the reader's mind.

The fiction writer revisits age-old issues. Love, loneliness, joy, misery, relationships, none of these are new, yet these are the raw material for stories of all types. In short, the doors a writer opens are ones that many have opened before, including the same writer. The novelty is not identifying the door but how it's traversed. Of importance is setting scenes for the reader to enter. In *Working* Robert Caro describes the importance of having *seen* for himself, having been there, where-ever that might be. Before starting his great biography of Lyndon Johnson, Caro spent days and nights alone in barely populated Johnson City, Texas, which made him understand the vast emptiness and loneliness in which Lyndon Johnson was raised. He then contrasted that scene with the majestic white marble columns and arches of the nation's Capitol dazzling and glittering in morning sun. In biography, such detail of setting allows the reader to understand the moods and feelings of the person there; in fiction, it allows the author to create the feelings of the character by placing the reader there.

When writing fiction or science writers and scientists both seek new doors to open – paths to follow – but their different methods are reflected in their writing. As a scientist I needed to explain each experimental step in full and consider alternative interpretations and implications, leaving as little as possible for the reader to question. Proper referencing to previous work of my own and others was critical, and whatever was new needed detailed explanation; the goal was always clarity. A well-written science article, like a realistic painting, attends to every detail, with care to not include what's not there. A scientist captures an audience by pointing to new doors to open and speculating on the landscapes on the other side of that opened door.

Each question a scientist asks is potentially a new door, which may be opened or ignored. If opened, it almost always leads to more new doors. After discovering genetic switches that activate genes in the eye lens, for example, we could have investigated possible clinical applications, a new path to follow. Instead, we left that door closed and studied how the switch evolved, also a new door to open. The doors I chose to open made all the difference in the direction of my research. If I'd opened a clinical door, I would have ended in a hospital setting. By opening a basic science door, I found myself in the mangrove swamp of Puerto Rico studying jellyfish.

Clichés

At the first meeting of Joyce Maynard's writing workshop that I attended in Lake Atitlan, Guatemala, she said, stressing the importance of creativity in writing, "Always avoid clichés." Then she read a few passages written by the participants pointing out unwanted clichés that should be replaced with more descriptive and original phrases. When she got to my writing, she singled out my use of "neat" to describe an idea that my protagonist had in a draft of a short story. I hadn't considered that one word, neat, would be a cliché. She made me more aware of each word or phrase or jargon of any sort. It also got me thinking about clichés in general.

I get it. Clichés are frowned upon as unimaginative and superficial, such as "a picture is worth a thousand words." Clichés are dull. Boring. Lazy. Banal. Readers and writers cringe at whatever they consider a cliché. I remember when a friend read a short story I wrote and said that I needed to delete "the fire crackled," since it was a cliché. If I read a cliché or two in the first chapter of a book, I often think, perhaps too quickly, that the book is not worth my time. Movies, plays, or any form of entertainment also suffer from overused themes or ways of depicting subjects. A friend of mine walked out of the movie "Black Swan" complaining that it was nothing but a cliché of the ballet world. I'm not sure cliché was the perfect word for what he meant, but in any case, I didn't agree. There you are: a cliché to one person may not be to another.

Another problem with clichés is that they conveniently bypass the need for thought or justification. Senator Lindsay Graham repeated "actions speak louder than words" – a cliché that's "old as the hills" – as an attempt to excuse President Trump's lies without going into the damning details. Most would agree with Graham's cliché that acts trump words, without considering that words sometimes inspire, teach and elevate more effectively than acts. By being such common knowledge, Graham's cliché eliminated the need for explanation or details. What were the acts, why were those acts important, and what acts were not performed? Because clichés are so commonly accepted, they substitute for the acts. It's easy to forget that clichés are only metaphors, not reality, and thus they often mislead.

But at times clichés have their uses. A writer can create low-brow, uneducated characters by having them use a string of clichés. And what about an eight-year-old bullied by his or her sibling and say, "Sticks and stones will break my bones, but words will never hurt me." I accept that cliché as a child's retaliation against bullying, even though words can and do hurt.

What about potential clichés that have important origins? Consider Theodore Roosevelt's, "Speak softly and carry a big stick." The power of that phrase guided government policy. Winston Churchill inspired a nation in wartime, possibly saving civilization, when he said, "I have nothing to offer but blood, toil, tears and sweat." Potential clichés such as these may be worth repeating in various contexts, with proper referencing of course. We admire Shakespeare because of his prose and poetry, much of which could now be considered clichés: Hamlet's, "To be or not to be," and Falstaff's, "Discretion is the better part of valor." These evocative phrases capture human nature in a few concise words. Similarly, the phrase "survival of the fittest," referring to Darwin's evolution, perhaps overused to the extent of becoming a cliché (and not always true) remains sufficiently important to be applied in other contexts. I call such phrases potential clichés that matter. Words matter in all their forms: spoken and unspoken, conscious and unconscious, honest and dishonest, even clichés at times.

Once upon a time, I walked into a charming new shop called *Shelf Indulgence Used Book Boutique* (clever name) in Sarasota. One of the owners was on the porch wrapping books in brown paper and writing on the wrapping. I asked her why she was doing that.

"Making blind dates for curious readers," she said.

What? Blind dates? For books?

I went inside to check out the store. There was a stand with a number of wrapped books, each containing a few statements on the wrapper to kindle my curiosity. I picked one that seemed intriguing (murder, legal thriller, best-selling author). No cover photo or blurbs, only wrapping with teasers on the front, not even the author's name. Was this page-turner by John Grisham about a murder committed to save lives of others ? The story could be riveting, or it could be...well, nothing special. *Don't judge a book by its cover.*

Curiosity and imagination trumped information, and so I bought one of the books to find out. Isn't that often how it works today? At least for me. We have information overload for just about everything, and so we retreat into our own head and take a chance on a "blind date." A blind date book is an ingenious idea. More power to this creative store.

Oh, I should mention, I didn't like the book after reading a few chapters and discarded it.

Sensitivity Readers

On the front page of the New York Times (December 24, 2017), Alexandra Alter advanced the merits of so-called sensitivity readers, who look for underlying prejudices or misunderstandings in books and articles that might have unintended consequences. Sensitivity readers screen for slurs, discrimination or ignorance of cultural realities for the purpose of removing inadvertent bias or prejudice or simply erroneous interpretations due to lack of knowledge, especially when authors write outside of their expertise. A rabbinical student screening a book by a Hindu author about a Jewish orthodox wedding would be an example of a situation a sensitivity reader would tackle trying "to anticipate blind spots before they ignite full-blown social media conflagrations." Sensitivity readers are sought especially for children's books, which can influence young minds in formative and impressionable stages.

Alter did warn how sensitivity readings could approach censorship or lead to homogenized literature. The defense against censorship was that "sensitivity readers aren't preventing authors from tackling tough subjects or writing cross-culturally but helping to guard against misrepresentations."

Although it's hard to disagree with the benefits of a sensitivity reader, and I'm all for rigorous editing – for legal, cultural, technical or literary reasons – my initial reaction was negative. I wondered what bothered me, since I'm certainly not an advocate of prejudice or against correcting honest mistakes. My problem was the word "sensitivity" being used as a sweetener to remove any possible bitter taste of the text, a whisper to the author and publisher and ultimately reader that reading for sensitive issues will make the book neutral, correct, sanitized and without bias. But, what of opinions not shared by everyone, such as many social, political or religious issues?

Confounding literary editing or screening for issues that could lead to lawsuits with the concept of sensitivity raises troubling issues for me. Isn't literature supposed to expose as much as to inform? Do children benefit by reading books whitewashed from uncomfortable situations or points of view – including prejudice – which they may encounter from their diverse peers or social situations? Isn't there a role for parental or teacher guidance for this for children? Is protection well served by avoidance or censorship of too much? Aren't the best books the ones that acknowledge conflict, injustice and raw truth by showing, even between the lines, rather than those that give a vanilla taste to bitter herbs?

Cultural norms are seldom shared, and those of one group may be offensive to another group: should those norms be blotted out of books? And what about the evolution of prevalent norms and prejudices over time? Offensive words or views can become acceptable over time. Movies and television and books today are filled with dialogue such as, "What the fuck?" That's no longer taboo in the same way as it was yesterday. Which brings up just when was "yesterday?" We don't know what contentious words, events or ideas today will be accepted tomorrow. Might the representation of prejudice be a quicker route for its extinction than its avoidance by sensitivity readers?

For sure bias and bigotry are reprehensible and reinforce undesirable social trends. Prejudice permeates culture as cancer cells metastasize bodies. Think of anti-Semitic or anti-Muslim or racist comments. I caution, however, against selected readers using subjective criteria of cultural sensitivity, an ambiguous concept that opens the lid for the propagation of the viewpoints of the sensitivity readers rather than those of the authors. There is a fine line between helpful literary editing, censorship and manipulating opinions.

Sensitivities vary with individuals and change over time. It wasn't long ago that a sensitivity reader would have targeted gay or interracial marriage. Books, like art, are valuable cultural histories, as genes and fossils are imprints of evolution from which we trace our identity.

When Is Enough?

When to end a creative project, when to stop refining or polishing and when to draw the conceptual line ending the venture? I'm driven to rewrite, add or delete a word here, rephrase a sentence there. It's an incessant quest for perfection that doesn't exist and brings to mind the cliché, *perfection is the enemy of good.* A more substantive difficulty is finding the line that marks the end of the project. When was my science project complete enough to publish? When to put the final period on a short story or novel? Frans Kafka never did for *The Castle,* which ended in the middle of a sentence. When was my Inuit art collection comprehensive enough to stop collecting? "Never," was my chronic answer, in spite of not wanting to emulate Madeline Kripke; she died in her Greenwich Village apartment with 20,000 dictionaries, an extreme example of the never-ending, obsessive quest for collecting (New York Times, May 1, 2020).

The nagging frustration of when to end a creative project came up when I heard Jeffrey Goldberg speak about his timely article, "The Obama Doctrine," in *The Atlantic.* James Bennet, editor of the magazine, questioned Goldberg about his extensive interviews with President Obama. Goldberg explained that his objective was not so much to analyze Obama's future legacy, but to gain a greater insight into his mind and how he reasoned to solve problems. When Bennet asked Goldberg what Obama's doctrine was, Goldberg concluded that Obama was an intelligent pragmatist who centered his thinking on the world as it is, not as he would like it to be, and concluded his philosophy was "pragmatic restraint."

I took note of a side comment that Goldberg muttered under his breath numerous times when responding to queries from the audience. After answering the best that he could, he said, half-aloud, as if to himself, "I should have written more about that." Never mind that this was one of the longest articles ever published in *The Atlantic*. From Goldberg's viewpoint, the article wasn't complete enough. The complexity of the subject outweighed the article; Obama's pragmatic restraint was no more than a term, not the restraint itself, and explanation couldn't substitute for original thoughts and acts. Was Goldberg not satisfied with the article or with himself for not going deeper? How much deeper?

It appears as if Leonardo Da Vinci struggled to find a satisfactory end to his paintings. He worked *very* slowly, taking years to finish, and often leaving his work unfinished. He used layers upon layers of paint, some transparent, to give a three-dimensional perspective to his work, and developed innovative styles, such as sfumato for example, with softened edges and color transitions that mimicked human vision of what's in and out of focus. He worked on *Mona Lisa* for seventeen years and died at 67 with it in his bedroom, along with other masterpieces, which were never delivered as promised. Did he just not want to part with *Mona Lisa*, or did he feel there was more to do, that it wasn't finished? Was he going to add more mystery to her subtle smile? Leonardo never stopped experimenting with his many innovations, always modifying and improving. Perhaps such genius can only be admired, not copied, but what better example for the difficulty of accepting when the finish line has been crossed for creativity at its zenith.

Many of his greatest works (for example, *Adoration of the Magi* and *Saint Anne)* were what Walter Isaacson calls in his biography of Leonardo, "unfinished perfections." What a wonderful concept, unfinished perfection, finishing as an illusion for any truly creative act. Even what we may call perfect is still unfinished, since there's always more that could be done, small changes that might improve the work. Limiting boundaries are impossible to maintain in any creative undertaking, for each door that's opened leads into more rooms with more doors to open, in an endless parade of possibilities. Unfinished means there is still room for imagination and experimentation, which there always is, so it's up to the artist to accept, for whatever reason, it is time to stop.

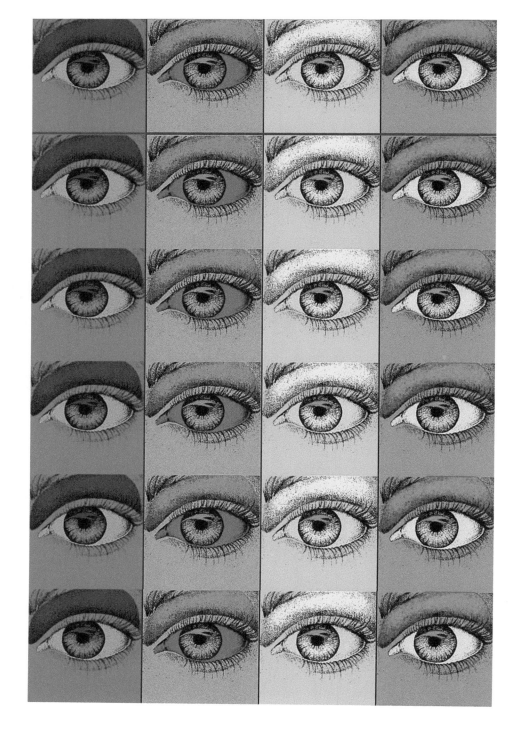

COLLECTING

Inuit Art

My Inuit art collection started by chance and sprouted into a passion. It started after a day's skiing with my family in Vail when I was strolling along the busy main street and passed a gallery, The Alaskan Shop, with beautifully shaped sculptures displayed in the window. The sculptures were made from natural products of the Arctic: green serpentine stones and black stones and caribou antlers and walrus tusks and musk ox horns and whalebone. I was struck by the incredible movement inherent in the carvings, as if they were alive. Dazzled and curious, I ambled into the gallery, where I felt surrounded by dozens of dancers. These weren't souvenirs, as I've heard Eskimo and Inuit art described; they were fine art. I picked up a small marine ivory bear, prowling, with beady black eyes and fine scratches along its body giving the impression of fur. The owner saw that I connected with that little bear and smiled.

Although I didn't buy any sculptures, the bear clung to my mind when I got home.

Perhaps its soul had seeped into me. I called the gallery's owner, bought it, and it became my first sculpture from the Arctic. I had yet to appreciate the difference between that Alaskan bear and Inuit art from Arctic Canada.

I received my first Inuit sculpture – a kneeling caribou in green serpentine stone – as a 50th birthday present from my son, Anton. Soon thereafter, I acquired a lively, dark-stoned drum dancer looking skyward by Luke Airut from Igloolik. Luke Airut? I'd never heard of him. Igloolik? That was off my radar. I had no idea that it was a hamlet on Igloolik island north of the Arctic Circle in the Inuit territory of Nunavut. Sculptures by Michelangelo or Henry Moore or any number other iconic artists are well-known, fill museums and are the subject of innumerable books. Inuit artists from the remote Arctic belonged to a different breed filled with mystery. Part of my excitement about Inuit sculptures was discovering these treasures in the shadows of a new world.

Historically, the Inuit carved small stone, bone or ivory amulets for hundreds of years. The Canadian artist, James Houston, visited the Arctic and was impressed by their remarkable carvings, which he collected and used to introduce Inuit sculptures to the public by organizing a major exhibit in Montreal in 1949 at the Canadian Handicrafts Guild (today called The Canadian Guild of Crafts or La Guilde). The exhibition was a resounding success and provided the foundation for commercial Inuit art. Houston went on to live in the Arctic for many years and played a key role developing the field of Inuit art by encouraging the Inuit to be authentic and making their art accessible to those outside of the Arctic. He also went to Japan to learn and then teach printmaking to the Inuit. He was beloved by the Inuit, who called him Saumik, meaning the left-handed one.

I began to collect Inuit sculptures bit by bit while learning from books and Inuit art dealers who became my friends: John Burdick in Washington, DC and Harold Seidelman in Toronto. It didn't take long to discover that these magnificent works were a microcosm with values I held dear and a culture that was new to me. In brief, Inuit art comprised the centrality of family, groups and cooperation; playfulness, sports and humor; throat singing and response to music; ancient legends and myths; and spirits and spiritual beliefs. The many sculptures of shaman were chimeras of humans and various animals, perhaps a bird with a human face or even a whale with caribou antlers – transformations into part animal, part human – sharing their respective powers. This appealed to me as a scientist interested in evolution, for all species of the animal world, including humans, are cousins, and the Inuit expressed this with skill, uncanny intuition and imagination in their art.

An especially interesting aspect of Inuit art to me was the unexpected diversity from a homogeneous, frigid environment dark as night for much of the year. I loved how the artists weaved together aesthetically their lifestyle with stories and legends, giving each piece multiple dimensions. Also, many of their sculptures are of similar animals – bears, musk ox, caribou, birds, seals – or common themes – mother/child, the Sedna myth (see below), shaman – yet each carving had a distinct style, such as realistic, abstract or surreal. In the same way that one can recognize a Van Gogh painting or Giacometti sculpture from afar – both household names among artists – one can recognize a sculpture by Ennutsiak or Davidialuk or Pangnark or Talirunuili, or many other Inuit artists by its style as well as subject. That the voices of the Inuit artists trump the subject matter was, for me, an important ingredient of their creativity.

Except for the rare Inuit art collector, I never met anyone who could name a single Inuit artist (granted that their names are sometimes almost unpronounceable!) or was aware of the diversity and artistic importance of Inuit art. Thus, collecting these art treasures was in keeping with my penchant for doing research on scallop and jellyfish eyes, which even few scientists know have sophisticated eyes with striking similarities, as well as fascinating differences, to our own eyes. Like my scientific research, then, collecting Inuit art became an adventure in an obscure, foreign territory.

Some years ago, when I went to the Houston North Inuit Gallery in Nova Scotia run by Alma Houston, the ex-wife of James Houston, a carving of a swimming bear by Axangyu Shaa from Cape Dorset, Baffin Island, glanced in my direction. Alma noticed my interest in the bear and came to me. After some small talk she said, caressing its back, "There's just something about this piece that *feels* right." Her words carried weight since she had lived in the Arctic with her husband and was a link between the inanimate sculpture and the living force behind its creation. I ran my palm gently down the bear's back as she had. It "felt right" to me as well and I bought it.

Touching magically melted a boundary and allowed me to blend with the art. How often have we touched, or needed to restrain our desire to touch, a sculpture or other object or person? I remember when my father died, my mother placed my hand on his body to make me understand that he was dead. Touching created a tangible reality that was unachievable by sight alone. Touching lets us escape our own tiresome universe and enter that of the artist's sphere for a few precious moments; it enhances our appreciation of a rich patina generated by aging, and awakens the spirits of many others who caressed and admired the art before us. In a word, touching humanizes the inanimate stone sculpture. When Helen Keller famously placed her hand on the violin being played by the incomparable Jascha Heifetz and felt its vibrations to "hear" the music, she declared that touch was the most important sense.

The limited senses available to this remarkable lady, who was blind and deaf, must have made her appreciate the wonders of touch far more than we do, where touch is diluted by sight and sound, an irony that fits with the advantage of limited variables to gain insight. Sculpture is born to be touched, and I often handle my Inuit carvings as I admire them and ask my guests to do the same.

Looking at my collection, it is not evident how it was acquired and assembled, but the process for each piece occupies a nook of space in my memory. Even a minor piece can have greater personal meaning depending upon where and how I acquired it. For example, after I'd decided to purchase the swimming bear in Alma Houston's gallery, my eyes drifted to other carvings like a child in a toy store. When I couldn't decide between two which had captured my attention, Alma pointed to the carving by Lukta Qiatsuk from Cape Dorset, Baffin Island and said, "Buy this one. You'll never regret it." It was a mother owl with her baby chick clasped on her back, a common mother/child theme of Inuit art. The mother projected an alertness, providing security for her chick, whose head rested tenderly against her head. The black stone became soft feathers in my mind, a miraculous job of alchemy by the artist. I bought the sculpture. I think of Alma and appreciate its magic more every time I see it. But another factor is in play as well. If not for an appreciative viewer there would be only cut stone, no emotion, nothing transmitted. Such is the responsibility and satisfaction of an art collector: to create a receptive home for the art.

Later, as I skimmed through a book, *Lords of the Stone*, Alma had given me, I was conscious of how much I had yet to learn about the diversity and mythology of Inuit art. Little knowledge can be more daunting than ignorance. As I paged through the book, I felt like an adventurer approaching a mountain, which looked more formidable the closer I came to the base. The challenge of learning enough has always taunted me to fully appreciate my Inuit art collection, as it also drove me as a scientist. Both collecting Inuit art and scientific research have made me enlarge, modify and reevaluate my views and ideas, leaving no time for boredom or justification for conceit.

As might be expected, I was excited about every new piece of Inuit art that I bought, but the acquisition was a stranger at first; it takes time for a new friend or even a new baby freshly home from the hospital to become familiar. As time goes by, the excitement gives way to the deeper sense of the art joining my family in its own right. It's always especially heartwarming when I visit my children's homes and am greeted by a piece of art I have lived with and is now theirs as a bonified member of their family. It's the whisper of private voices from the art to me that moves it from the mind to the heart.

I was impressed with the depth of the reciprocal relationships of art to its owner when a group of Inuit art curators and scholars from Canada visited my collection.

"Oh, there's the mother and child carving my parents owned when I was growing up," said one, as he stood transfixed before it. He had just met a sibling after many years of absence.

"There's my father's friend," said another, as he looked at a photograph of an Inuit covered with pelts of white foxes on my wall. "I know his carvings too."

"I'm so glad this small piece is part of your collection," said a member of the group, who owns a gallery and knew the artist. "It's safe here."

Art's private voice is as powerful and personal as its public persona.

My collection of Inuit art has grown for over 30 years. I exhibited 34 pieces, which gave some sense of the breadth of Inuit art at the World Bank in Washington, DC in 2018. To give a flavor of this unique ethnic art, I show here a smattering of pieces from my collection.

SELECTED SCULPTURES

Luke Iksitaaryuk's sculpture of four Inuit captures physical movement and inner determination. The first in line trudges along slightly ahead of the group, looking around, maybe for the best path to take. The figures also suggest an outing of friends on a sunny day in the tundra. Pure guesswork, but isn't that a key challenge of art, to interpret and relate the art to one's own thoughts, feelings and dreams?

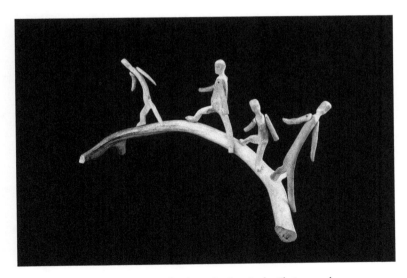

(*Walking Figures*; Caribou Antler; Luke Iksitaaryuk; Baker Lake; Early 1970s)

Osuitok Ipeelie's sculpture of a caribou walking while sniffing the air blends realism with visual poetry.

(*Caribou*; Serpentine, Caribou Antler;
Osuitsok Ipeelee; Cape Dorset, Baffin Island)

Oviloo Tunnillie's moving sculpture of a grieving mother was no doubt inspired by the suicide of the artist's daughter.

(*Grief*; Serpentine; Oviloo Tunillie; Cape Dorset, Baffin Island)

John Attok's expressive sculpture shows a son leading his infirm father to freeze to death on an ice flow. In the past, such sad events occurred occasionally when an elder could no longer contribute to the struggle for life and became a burden. We view this with horror, however the Inuit belief in an afterlife no doubt softened the blow for them. In addition, escape from the cruelties of old age allowed death with dignity for the benefit of the family.

(*Son Leading Father to Die*; Grey Stone;
John Attok; Arviat; 1965 – 1970)

Tuteeya Ikkidluak's magnificent sculpture portrays a hunter/fisherman as a dancer balanced with technical ingenuity.

(*Hunter*; Serpentine, Caribou Antler; Cord; Tuteeya Ikkidluak; Cape Dorset, Baffin Island; 1978)

John Pangnark, a pioneer in Inuit abstraction, carved many abstract shapes the individual Inuk. This sculpture shows the typical face of this artist's carvings. It comprises no more than a few faint scratches. The sculpture offers mere suggestions of the anatomical structures.

(*Man with Outstretched Arms*; Black Stone; John Pangnark; Arviat; Year not Known)

John Tiktak's sculpture of a head has a Mona Lisa-like ambiguity. Is he/she smiling, smirking, lost in thought? The slight upward curve of the mouth brings this carving to life.

(*Head*; Dark Brown Stone;
John Tiktak; Rankin Island; 1968)

David Reuben's sculpture of a shaman blends man and flying bird. Shaman are intermediaries with magical powers, including those of animals, which travel between the human and spiritual world. The relative proportions of different species vary in different transformation sculptures of shaman. These chimeras clearly do not comply with scientific rules of evolution established by genetics and fossils. As a scientist interested in evolution, however, transformation pieces represent artistically at a single time point the interrelationship of all species, humbling the idea of the superiority of any one species. I love it.

(*Bird Shaman*;
Brazilian Soapstone;
David Reuben; Paulatuk/
Toronto; Year not Known)

Abraham Pov's starkly elegant Sedna shows her providing fish. Of the many Inuit myths, that of the Sedna (mermaid) is arguably the most important. There are various Sedna legends. According to one, the Sedna originated from an unhappily married woman who lived on an island with her evil husband. The girl's father, who had given permission for her to marry the man, went with his kayak to the island to rescue her. Furious after discovering that his wife had been kidnapped, her husband transformed into a bird, flew to the retreating kayak and flapped his wings to create waves. The rough sea threatened to capsize the small boat, so her father tossed his daughter overboard to save himself (not exactly a loving paternal act) and worse, chopped off pieces of her fingers as she clung to the side of the boat (ugh!). But here's the miracle: she sank to the bottom and transformed into the revered Sedna, and the pieces of her fingers gave rise to the marine mammals. The Sedna became responsible for providing seafood for the Inuit people and, ultimately, the source of many other things. Sedna, the provider, has been a major focus of Inuit art.

(*Sea Goddess Holding Fish*; Dark Grey Stone; Abraham Pov; Povungnituk, Baffin Island; Year not Known)

Bill Nasogaluak's sculptures make social statements. An example is a seal going through a barrel of oil, protesting the pollution of the oceans.

(*Seal in Oil Barrel*; Brazilian Soapstone; Bill Nasogaluak; Tukoyatuk/Toronto; Year not Known)

Objects

Space for new acquisitions is a perennial problem for collectors, especially collectors of sculpture. Objects! There was a postdoctoral fellow in my laboratory who said he never wanted to own anything more than could fit in his car. (He didn't tell me the size of his car.) He considered objects – especially possessions – quicksand. "First they trap you, then they suck you under," he said.

He had a point. Possessions need attention and are laden with responsibilities and expenses, such as insurance and other protective measures, as well as upkeep. It is a short step from owning objects to being owned by them. I even knew a man who refused to own a car and went everywhere by taxi. "It's easier and cheaper," he said. "No need to buy gasoline, make repairs or buy insurance. No charges for garage space or parking. No traffic violations or risk of accidents."

He had my full attention; my fender-bender was in repair at the moment.

We are a culture fond of stuff, possessions we enjoy as well as those that burden us. But many items have benefits. Vehicles give mobility, homes provide a safe haven, books enlighten, art taps a magical spot, indulgences provide pleasure. But what about my collecting? Should I limit myself to an arbitrary number of Inuit sculptures? I know a collector who would never own more than 30 pieces; for each after that he would get rid of one. Can I justify accumulating more and more?

Maybe.

Consider the personal, existential aspect of objects, as brilliantly related in the novel *The Museum of Innocence* by Turkish Nobel laureate, Orphan Pamuk. Kemal falls in love with Füsun, his distant shopgirl cousin, however she marries someone else. Eventually she divorces, becomes engaged to Kemal, but tragically gets killed in an auto accident before they marry. To celebrate the times he spent with Füsun, Kemal collects objects she has touched that remind him of her – a saltshaker, a pen, the bedframe upon which they made love. These objects were not only infused with *her*, but also an extension of who *he* was.

Yes, I thought. My Inuit sculptures aren't just rocks carved by a stranger that fill my house, they are a part of me, an extension of who I am and project feelings of beauty and tenderness and humor and sadness without words. There are two types of revolutionaries: one builds monuments and the other destroys to make space to erect new ones. My nature is to build, not tear down. My growing collection – objects – is my creation, more than accumulated sculptures. My presence, as well as the collection, grows with every acquisition. No two collectors would amass the same collection: the collection becomes the collector. Each new piece fills a small space in the monument, makes it bolder, more complete, and adds a vital bit to the collection and to me. Ceasing to collect would be stunting my growth; dispensing with my sculptures would be an amputation.

The sculptures in my collection have many layers of meaning. These include the myths they represent, as well as the stories of their creators and their part in my own story, as a collector of these pieces. This is in addition to their aesthetic appeal – their shapes, expression, sense of movement and balance. In them, I see the echo of my own multifaceted life: the scientist who seeks natural truths; the artist who delves into the mysteries of human truths; the intuitive explorer who likes adventure; and the writer who imagines and fantasizes.

Boundaries

I have heard it said that true collectors, in contrast to those who just gather haphazardly, collect almost anything, but that's too broad for my taste. Most collections have boundaries, and these can be quite surprising. I know a person who collects buttons from 17th century French military uniforms! My friend Stanton collects anything to do with schnauzers, his favorite dogs. Although boundaries set limitations, they also expose buried features that enrich and reveal complexity. The diversity of Inuit artistic voices, bounded by their ethnicity, ranges from realistic to abstract and even pure fantasy. These are manifest in the sculptures of the same animals or similar themes, such as shamanism, family scenes, or mythological stories. A striking similarity exists in science. Limited variables reveal insights that couldn't be made by widespread comparisons. There is no better example than Charles Darwin's comparisons of the beaks of finches in the Galapagos Islands to illustrate the importance of small variations within a defined region as the crux of adaptation and evolution. The far-reaching idea of natural selection could not have come by comparing the beaks of finches with those of eagles or mouths of frogs.

Art within a restricted boundary also underscores the importance of context. Placing carvings by the same artists or those related by style or subject next to one another highlights their overlapping qualities and differences. I have an Inuit sculpture by Josiah Nuilaalik from Baker Lake showing a man lifting and carrying away a woman to be his bride. Both her head and his tilt upwards, their eyes focused on the heavens. When the sculpture stands alone on a shelf at eye level, it emphasizes the man's dominance, who seems to be thanking God for his good fortune. When placing the same sculpture on a low pedestal with the abducted fiancée looking up at a sculpture of a shaman, her plight grabs the attention. Perhaps she is begging for help, or maybe she's announcing, "Look at me; I'm getting married!" I often play with context like this – arrange and rearrange the placements of my Inuit carvings – searching for different meanings and artistic richness hidden in them.

A Singular Unit

My collection as a whole evolved into a personal, single sculptural artwork, and the collection – the collective artwork – changed its nature as new pieces entered my exclusive club. As the collection changed character, perhaps stressing more mythology or one artist over others, so did my tastes and boundaries and sub-boundaries that I had drawn. I depended to some extent on where it "felt right" and where it didn't, which members fit better in the collection or which had diminished prominence when compared with new additions. However, culling – tightening the boundary of excellence by deleting pieces considered "lesser" or had lost my affection (both reluctant, subjective feelings) – invariably left a sadness that made me question whether I'd been rash or disloyal to a family member.

Authenticity

The quagmire of authenticity – correct attribution – is one of the most difficult and important challenges of a collector. What a serious puzzle that can be! I'm not considering admitted reproductions: no one mistakes the person who documents a quotation for the original source. I'm talking about artwork acquired in good faith as authentic that becomes targeted as a reproduction. A fake. Not the real thing. Stealing. Equivalent to plagiarism in literature. I doubt there ever was a collector or curator who wasn't plagued by the question of authenticity. A major complicating factor is when authenticity becomes a matter of opinion that can vary for many reasons: insufficient evidence, politics, self-interest. Was the believed masterpiece in the collection really made by the specified artist, or was it the hand of a student under his or her direction? Or, heavens forbid, good gracious no, was it produced by a swindler who mimicked "the great one" to make a buck? One expert swears your artwork is as good as gold, but another is ambivalent and says that it has some elements of the real thing but, then again, it has other features that look questionable: the signature in the "wrong" place, the composition atypical for the artist, the brush strokes too thin. Another major collector who owns two important works by the same artist may declare with certainty yours is not authentic because it differs from his in some respect, as if the artist has only one style that never varies, or that the piece differs in some respect from another in a museum by the same artist. This know-it-all expert may carry powerful credentials and can poison the artwork for the market, whatever the elusive truth. One negative word inflicts more damage than a plethora of positives in the opinionated and subjective world of art. The same can be said of science. One harsh criticism by a panel member reviewing grants, which are critical to sustain the productivity of scientists, often overwhelms approval by other reviewers. Art, like proposed studies in science, must be enmeshed in the familiar to be recognized as authentic.

In addition to Inuit art, I collected tribal African art, which is harder to authenticate since the artists, provenance and history are largely unknown. An established collector in the field saw my collection of African art, and I foolishly asked for his opinion. I had far less knowledge about African art, a huge field compared to Inuit art.

"Since you ask," he said matter-of-factly after a cursory look, "most of these are reproductions."

Oh my god, stunned, dizzy, my pride brutalized, my confidence crippled. The blood drained from my head, and I had to sit down to gather my wits. After a moment, I wondered, what does he mean by "reproductions?" That they are not the first of a kind, or that they were made in the jungle years ago for trading purposes instead of tribal rituals, or that they were mass-produced recently for tourists? I was correct in fearing the last.

"I've seen centers in Africa where they mass produce tribal art and label it authentic," he said.

I knew they were not made recently since I'd bought them from a knowledgeable, life-long collector and gallery owner who had acquired many of them some fifty years ago. Regaining equanimity, I pointed to an early twentieth century Luba staff with conjoined female twins at the top from the Democratic Republic of Congo, and asked, "Why do you think this is a reproduction?"

"Well," he answered, with an arrogant tone of certainty, "it's a common theme."

Then I asked him why he questioned the authenticity of an early twentieth century Baga snake headdress known as a "Mantsho-na-Tshoi" from Guinea. These are made honoring boys coming of age, such as a Bar-Mitzvah would.

"I haven't seen one with a shape quite like that before," he answered, implying that he was familiar with everything that took place in tribal Guinea throughout its history. (The most outrageous comment that he made was that the breasts of a female figure on a Luba staff were too large!)

I wondered which of the two opinions against authenticity was more lethal: the *common* theme of the conjoined twins on the Luba staff or the *uncommon* shape of the Baga snake – commonality in one case and originality in the other. Didn't these reasons for dismissing authenticity contradict one another? But, then again, one or another of the criticisms *may* be correct; I emphasize, *may* be correct, but not necessarily.

I felt his off-hand dismissals of authenticity reduced me to a charlatan collector. Funny how art that I bought made by strangers is felt like an extension of myself. The full stories of these beautiful African art pieces, and they are beautiful with their aged patina and skillful carving, are almost impossible to know for certain – long live conjecture. But I was pleased when many pieces from the source of my collection exhibited in New York received a positive review by Holland Cotter, a noted critic for African art.

I don't disparage respect for authenticity. Knowing that the art came directly from the hand of the artist matters a great deal to me. A replica, no matter how skillful, creates a distance between the art and me, losing impact in the chasm, like weathering a hurricane in a movie instead of in nature. Doubt of authenticity weighs heavy and challenges me, as it does all collectors. I have tiptoed on the narrow ridge between "right" and "wrong" – between good judgment and poor judgment – between good luck and bad luck – and understood that preconceptions and earlier beliefs may be questioned, even shattered, at any moment. Despite apparent confidence at times, art collectors are vulnerable creatures.

Interestingly, Blake Gopnik, an art critic, argued in the New York Times (November 2013), in favor of fakes, defined as forged works similar in style to that of famous artists and sold falsely as authentic. Admitting that such forgeries are an economic crime, he questioned whether they are an aesthetic or artistic crime. Gopnik's point was that any work good enough to fool experts had much going for it and provided proof that the ideas and innovations of the forged art are what count, not just the hands of the artist. Gopnik wrote, "The faker could be considered a faithful assistant" of the forged artists "who happened to arrive after they'd died." Indeed, many art masterpieces were created in the famous artist's studio with the assistance of students and other skilled painters. I wonder what the reaction would be if a lesser artist's work were forged by a greater artist. Would that devalue the forged work or make it less significant than an original work by the artist?

"But wait," cautions the Devil's advocate in me, who prefers to puncture balloons than inflate them. "Why all this talk about significance and value? Aren't I collecting for a love of art? Isn't it enough that the art is moving or aesthetically pleasing or whatever it was that attracted me? Why discredit a work of art because the artist may not have been the person I thought? And what about the question of who "stole" what from whom? Hardly any creative work is entirely unique, just like new species don't pop up without a common ancestor in evolution. Most artists were influenced by, or even copied, works of other artists. Edgar Degas traced drawings of ballerinas from his own earlier drawings to fill his canvasses. Is only the original ballerina drawing authentic? Except in rare cases, superb art was produced in environments where groups strongly influenced each other: Michelangelo and the Italian Renaissance; Rembrandt and the seventeenth century Dutch Golden Age; Renoir and the impressionist movement. Japanese art influenced Van Gogh, and African art influenced Picasso, but no one considers them derivative artists. For that matter, does influence or advice by gallery owners, museum curators or other collectors make a collector "derivative" without an original voice?

Consider a 'drip painting' of Jackson Pollock. There's little power in someone else creating a chaotic design by dripping paint on a canvas. That Pollock conceived the concept and made the picture are crucial to its place in history, which Pollock recognized himself, as judged from what he said: "It doesn't make much difference how the paint is put on as long as something has been said. Technique is just a means of arriving at a statement." The echo of a statement cannot compete with its original author. The authentic – called autograph – stands as an original monument, both artistically and historically. Whether or not admired, authenticity traces directly to its original source, the artist, and makes the work unique. Moreover, for me, authenticity allows bonding, without deception, of feeling and meaning between the artist and viewer.

The most dramatic example of the importance and impact of authenticity is in the marketplace. After the Japanese collector Yusaku Maezawa bought Jean-Michel Basquiat's skull painting for $110.5 million at Sotheby's auction, he proudly posted on his Instagram account, "I am happy to announce that I just won this masterpiece. When I first encountered this painting, I was struck with so much excitement and gratitude for my love of art. I want to share that experience with as many people as possible." Maezawa planned to exhibit the painting in a museum in his hometown of Chiba, Japan, after it travels internationally for a widespread audience.

I wonder if Maezawa would have bought this painting if there were any question about its authenticity, or if a colleague of Basquiat had been the artist? Would the same painting now be worth only a few thousand dollars at most, like it was a few years earlier, instead of the millions it went for?

The high price Maezawa paid elevated the authentic Basquiat to the same league as Picasso and other superstars in the marketplace and must have frustrated curators for not having acquired a Basquiat painting for their museum when it was affordable. After the auction, purchasing a Basquiat would be financially prohibitive. It seems not right that a few collectors with deep pockets set the market value for art, and thereby also establish its artistic importance.

There are collectors who own valuable paintings but display copies in their home and put the authentic pieces in a vault for protection. Apparently, they derive pleasure from knowing they own the original art, or maybe for them it's an investment rather than enriching their life by living with the authentic work. Do they get the same pleasure from the replica as from the original? I doubt they would if they didn't also own the original. I have often asked myself why an original work should be valued so outrageously high – made into a shrine – while an indistinguishable, exact copy, or a similar work by an unknown artist be relatively ignored? I agree that the Basquiat painting is impressive, but how much of the $110.5 million is hype, marketing and snobbism exacerbated by society?

Ambiguity

Ambiguity differs from authenticity. While authenticity questions *who* and has an external answer; ambiguity asks *what* it means and flounders in uncertainty. Authenticity requires investigation to establish the original source; ambiguity, by contrast, has no final answer and will vary with the viewer. It's inherent in the work itself. Ambiguity, uncertainty, can be central to the significance of the piece of art. It's about the complexity of life and extends to the factual world of science. Think of the uncertainty principal: is an electron a wave or a particle? Both are true; it depends on conditions. How's that for factual ambiguity?

Surprisingly, ambiguity can have a greater impact than certainty. Would Leonardo Da Vinci's "Mona Lisa" be as fascinating if it was obvious that she was smiling, or why, if we knew she was disappointed, or perhaps just posing for the master artist? I don't think so. Mona Lisa looks out at us, muddled with the ambiguity of human nature. Or, consider Franz Kafka, the master of ambiguity. Would *The Trial* have the same power if we knew that Joseph K did or didn't commit a crime and, if he did, what the crime was?

Ambiguity haunts us in uncertainty. For me, ambiguity is at the heart of creativity and a powerful magnet that draws us into the art, which never ends its search for truth. Unlike authenticity, ambiguity demands more than one possible answer and takes us on journeys that force us to explore our own life and views rather than only those of the artist. If I'm told the meaning, I listen; if I'm asked the meaning, I become part of the answer.

Similarities

Difficulty arises when I'm drawn to a piece of art that resembles one that I have in my collection, either by the same or different artist. How many similar pieces should I have in my collection when I like them all? What's the role of "repetitions" in a collection? I put "repetitions" in quotation marks because I don't mean exact copies. I mean versions. I'm considering pieces that are similar in style and subject.

Similarities could be considered redundant and, in that sense, unimaginative. Yet, I don't propose that every piece in a collection should be one of a kind. Small variations on the theme or style are often creative and reveal complexity, even if they have only small differences from the others, perhaps in hair style or eye width or eye width or facial features. A slight tilt of a sculpted or painted head can make it a different piece of art altogether from one without the tilt.

Slightly different perspectives of the same subject can also create significantly different works of art. Claude Monet's haystacks at different times of the day are a famous example. Vincent van Gogh's multiple versions of the postman Joseph Roulin are among his masterpieces. It's only by repeated examination of the same subject under slightly different conditions with small tweaks here and there that one can recognize the power of perspective and begin to understand the many choices that the artist had to make in creating the work. Rarely do the best efforts erupt at first or spontaneously.

Similar pieces can also be like buried mini-collections – siblings – wonderful additions both intellectually and artistically. For example, I have ten Alaskan carved ivory pipes from the late nineteenth century, which were made principally to trade with whalers. Each pipe is beautiful, some with different carved arctic animals along the top, and all are covered with artistic scrimshaw drawings of scenes of marine life and the Eskimo lifestyle. Some pipes are complex, while others are simple in design. Only when viewed together as a group does the dynamic culture and artistic productivity of Alaskan art become evident.

For me, similarities are not lacking in imagination; only collectors who don't recognize the artistic value of the variations of similar pieces are lacking in imagination. Thus, the paradox: unique art and important concepts can emerge from similarities.

Courage to Collect

Collecting art requires the courage to risk being ridiculed, sometimes for poor taste, sometimes for poor judgment, sometimes for being too impulsive. Consider auctions. After being attracted to an art piece being auctioned, I vet it the best I can, but ultimately, it's up to me to decide whether or not to take a chance. If the estimated value is reasonable, I imagine owning the piece and my heart rate increases as the auction progresses. The bidding escalates to the estimated value, and then the problem begins. Many collectors (not all) set a price they will not exceed even if they could afford to go higher, a disciplined business approach based on estimated worth and love for a bargain. But what if I can afford to go higher and my mind's eye sees the piece filling a gap in my collection, or I think it's exceptional and I simply want it, greedy as that may be? Clearly, a stone shaped with tools or a canvas covered with paint has no intrinsic value. While the immediate commercial value is estimated by precedence, the auction can establish a new precedence, like an unexpected scientific discovery can alter the path of research. Setting a record auction price for a given artist may be a bold, profitable act.

But what if the bidding continues to climb? Do I risk the consequences of challenging the marketplace? Are ignorant collectors with deep pockets driving up the bids or are knowledgeable collectors competing for the same valuable prize? The faint line between being a visionary and a fool, exploited by clever dealers, looms before me, but I must decide in seconds whether to bid higher or let the opportunity, and the art piece, vanish. My hands moisten and I battle doubts. But if the final bid is mine, even if over expectation, I'm happy to see my collection advance another step. Or does it? Maybe not always. The prize may seem a little less over time and the rigor mortis of remorse may set in for having been too impulsive. I find it unconvincing when a collector claims to be driven strictly by rationale rather than...than what? The chase? Obsession? I stake my claim, sometimes with anxiety, sometimes with exuberance, with no destination to reach or rules that must be followed.

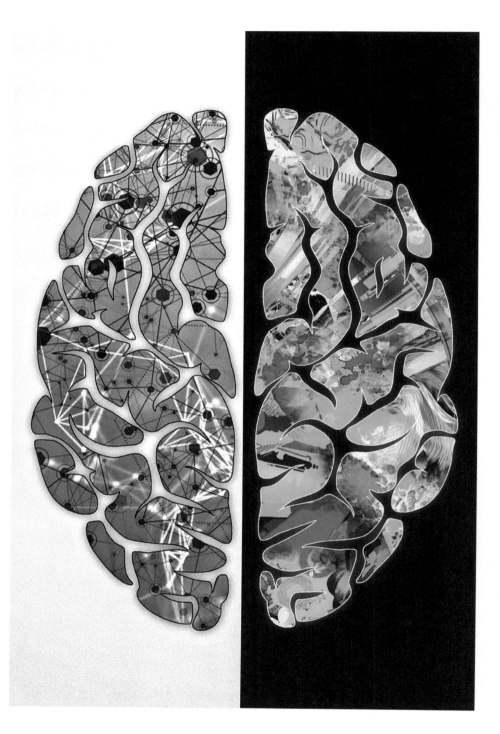

BRAINS

Computerizing Brains

Being a slow reader, I've dreamed of linking my brain to a book; in computer lingo, downloading books into my brain, wirelessly, of course. Imagine the time saved! I could get through *War and Peace* in less than an hour. Bookstores would become like fuel to download rather than an overwhelming challenge to select a book and read as many as I have time for.

"Brains aren't computers," warns the Devil's advocate lodged in the recesses of my mind, not at all happy with my idea. "Even if you could download a book into your brain, it would take the enjoyment out of reading and savoring your favorite passages."

Wrong on all counts, I counteract. Brains aren't less capable than computers, we just know less about them. We're still in the infancy of understanding the brain. If a book were downloaded into my mind instead of stored on a shelf, I could retrieve – perhaps by two blinks of my left eye as an innovative double-click – any passage or information I desired. Wouldn't that be wonderful! The book would become an internal part of me, a compartment of my modular brain, not just an external source. I could dance within the plot and party with the characters any time I wanted. No more tedium at boring occasions. Think of the advantage. Just last night, Lona and I met, unexpectedly, one of the most boring couple I know. Thank goodness for Lona, who has much more patience than I have and carried on the conversation, while I stood nodding now and then as if engaged. If only I could have read a downloaded book at the tip of my neurons!

"How's that different from simply using a smart phone or kindle or iPad?" persists the annoying Devil's advocate, determined to prove me wrong.

Well, I could lose an electronic device or not have it with me when I want to read or find the battery has died. Anyway, could I really whip out an iPhone and start reading anytime I wanted to? It's not subtle. Electronic devices glare when in use, and, frustratingly, seem to have a mind of their own. They only work well when they feel compliant.

Okay, science fiction is one thing, reality another. Still... I can't stop wishing for more, although I admit that I haven't exploited to the fullest or understand what I have already. I'm baffled how it's possible to transmit a manuscript halfway around the planet in seconds, or how a satellite thousands of miles away can beam information into my car to tell me what street I'm on and then lead me like a child step by step, or rather street by street, to any destination I choose. I'm lost in the present as if I were a stranger in a future world. I don't need to go back to college; I need to return to kindergarten. I'm stuffed to the brim with a ten-course meal, yet I'm asking for a candy bar.

"You're hopeless," mutters the Devil's advocate. "You sound like a politician who claims the moon when he can't help the Earth."

I confess, I lack a neutral gear and am stuck in overdrive. So be it. I am who I am, greedy for more perhaps, like it or not. Downloading information into my brain – a book or music or anything – and turning my brain into a computer warehouse is not enough. I dream of even more. Imagine this.

Linking Brains

A book is a finished product, a museum of old stuff, even if it touches on relevant issues. We turn pages to find out what the author already knows. In that sense a book is static, a done deal. But imagine how extraordinary if, instead of downloading what's known into our brains, we could eavesdrop into someone else's brain as it's working. Wirelessly again, of course, I'm not up for invasive brain surgery.

"Do you really want to know what someone else is thinking or have someone hack your brain? Wouldn't either be fatal for privacy?" The Devil's advocate is on a roll.

Good points. Learning the true thoughts of others could be devastating. Do I want to hear my family or friends, or anyone, say nasty things about me? Also, I wouldn't be able to hide my thoughts from them or anyone else. I'd need to bury my thoughts, lie to myself so convincingly, that I wouldn't even know my own truth. It might do away with truth altogether. Now, that's an interesting thought: a world without truth. Would scientists go out of business?

I'm letting the Devil's advocate of my own creation get the better of me. Linked brains wouldn't have to eliminate privacy. All that would be needed is a secure brain wi-fi communication.

And think of the benefits. Our brains are so isolated, encased in solid bone. They're orphans. We're always stuck in our own hermit brains and can easily mistake enemies for friends and friends for enemies. We really don't know anyone very well – even our family often surprise us. True, we may endanger privacy by linking brains to one another, but we would gain empathy and understanding. What a revolution that would be! We might finally be able to bridge gaps between us. On the other hand, if Jean-Paul Sartre is right and hell is "other people," linked brains might be the beginning of the end. Oh, the danger of progress, the uncertainty of life.

But why stop at person-to-person brain linkage? What about linking person-to-animal brains. I've always wanted to sense the world as an animal, to feel what it's like to *be* an animal. But which animal?

"It can't be done," says the Devil's advocate, echoing the pessimistic opinion of my science colleagues. "Our brains and those of animals are too different. Humans don't have the wiring to sense the world like any other species and we could never see or hear or feel the world like an animal; similarly, another species could never experience the world as humans do. Humans are even more isolated from the animal kingdom than our brains are from each other."

Oh, fiddlesticks, as my great grandparents may have said, in French or Russian, since that's where they were from. Our cat Mulligan used to dash off to who knows where chasing something or other in his mind. Exactly where or what? Mulligan teased our Bernese Mountain dog, Melanie, mercilessly by waving his paw under the sliver of space of the kitchen door until Melanie came around to inspect what that that was all about, only to get smacked on her nose. Melanie never caught on, stupid dog. But what was on Mulligan's mind? I would love to link directly into Mulligan's brain, to think like Mulligan, perhaps to learn from that imaginative and scheming cat.

And what about birds? The New York bestseller, *Alex & Me* by Irene Pepperberg, describes how her grey parrot, Alex, associated colors with shapes, apologized for misbehaving, teased people by playing games, demanded certain foods, acted as the boss, and more. That Alex had some form of "intelligence" seemed beyond dispute; only the nature of his intelligence remained obscure. Perhaps, then, I will be able to link my brain to a bird's brain to tap into that intelligence. If so, the question might switch to how my thoughts affect the bird's thoughts.

Charles Darwin's book, *The Expression of the Emotions in Man and Animals*, discusses many emotions – pain, pleasure, fear and others – showing similarities in expression in man and animals. Emotions blend into behavior and must be an outgrowth of thought, or perhaps it's the other way around: thought might be an evolutionary outgrowth of emotions. The ability to think couldn't have arisen spontaneously in humans. I presume that thinking must have evolved as any other trait, so successful linking a human brain to an animal brain might depend on which animal to use, at least at first, linking to the correct species. For that it's necessary to know the evolutionary pathways of thought, no different than comparing the proper fossils with the proper modern species.

"Maybe, and I stress *maybe*," whispers the Devil's advo-cate, the first sign of agreeing with me. "Primates, or dogs, or your cat Mulligan, may have some limited ability for abstract thought. I agree that there are signs that these mammals are more sophisticated than we give them credit for, and some brain linkage may eventually become possible. But evolution started way before them. Would you say that thinking started all at once in vertebrates, say fish?" asks the Devil's advocate, definitely more friendly.

What about invertebrates?

Intelligence

Don't short-change invertebrates too quickly. Humans assume the intelligence throne – the crown of superiority – even though we neither understand our own intelligence nor what it means for any animal. We compare how we think or reason with nothing, so to speak, since we have no idea how an animal thinks or reasons. We only say a dog or chimp, or any animal, shows some intelligence if it does something that seems human-like. Once my pet, Blooper, a mutt blended with an unknown number of dog strains, apparently jumped in the swimming pool (I'm convinced he slipped) and let a little girl hang on to him when she was splashing as if in trouble. From that day, Blooper was considered a genius. Believe me, Blooper was no genius! Yet, each species must have its unique form of intelligence. Wouldn't it be remarkable to sense 'an animal thought' in our linked brain?

I doubt any living thing could survive for millions of years in this threatening and often vicious world without some smarts. Some invertebrates appear unexpectedly brainy. *The Other Minds: The Octopus, the Sea, and the Deep Origins of Consciousness* by Peter Godfrey-Smith, a philosopher, tells about the surprising behavior of cephalopods. An octopus can learn to open a bottle by watching how another octopus does it. They show curiosity, have different moods – friendly, aggressive, timid – and can even engineer escape from their aquaria. *The Soul of an Octopus* by Sy Montgomery discusses additional complexity of these sea creatures, such as behavior indicative of befriending or disliking certain individuals, suggesting personality traits. Different animals sense the environment in alternate ways. We're not the only word on what the world is like.

There's even evidence that crayfish – small lobster-like crustaceans – have some mental activity. According to James Gorman's article, *What to Do When Crawdad Grows Anxious*, in the New York Times (June 12, 2014), crayfish in captivity roamed around periodically in the lighted part of an aquarium, possibly looking for bits of food. However, when a couple of French scientists, Pascal Fossat and Daniel Cattaert, subjected the crayfish to a mild electric shock, they stopped venturing from dark corners into the brightly lit areas. Why did these shocked, so-called brainless creatures, refuse to get out of the dark areas after the shock? It's a guess, of course, but it seemed like anxiety of some sort. The scientists injected the crayfish with a precursor to Valium called Librium, a drug used to treat anxiety in people, and the shocked crayfish started roaming around the bright spots again. Amazing, no? Crayfish behaved and responded pharmacologically like humans. Something interesting is going on that we don't understand. Maybe, just maybe, there's some kind of 'inner life' in these invertebrates. No doubt that crayfish brains are completely different from ours, but maybe they can also have similarities that can be linked to our brains. What's in a crayfish mind? I'd love to know.

Charles Darwin wrote a book on the behavior of the deaf and blind (but partly light-sensitive) earthworms, *The Formation of Vegetable Mould, Through the Action of Worms, with Observations on their Habits*. These clueless invertebrates grabbed triangular leaf bits, or pieces of paper, by the pointed ends more often than by the flat surfaces to drag them into their tubular burrows. Maybe this was fluke, but Darwin wrote, "It is…surprising that they apparently exhibit some degree of intelligence…in their manner of plugging up the mouths of their burrows. They act in nearly the same manner as would a man who had to close a cylindrical tube with different kinds of leaves…for they commonly seize such objects by their pointed ends."

Worm intelligence? I tend to draw the line here about linking my brain to an earthworm's, if I could even find it! Nonetheless, we are learning today what Darwin suspected almost 150 years ago: 'lower' animals are not that low. Perhaps his experiments on worms do indicate some type of intelligence in worms related to their environment and lifestyle. I think we'll change our view as we learn more about invertebrates, which get so little respect from us now. We'll swat an insect dead without the slightest qualm, treat it as no more than a leaf, despite the irony that we learned volumes about genetics that applies to humans from the fruit fly *Drosophila*. I'll risk saying that the short answer to whether invertebrates display intelligence of sorts is a qualified yes. They are very different from humans and other animals, but don't discard the role of adaptation to their environment, which has led to complex behavior consistent with an intelligence that works for them.

Language

My friend John Burdick told me that Daniel Dennett, a philosopher, considered language the primary difference between humans and other species. Really? Would that prohibit person to animal brain linkage?

Although I had not read anything by Dennett, I objected to this simplified view. My problem was that animals have their own language just like they have their own intelligence: octopus change colors and patterns quickly, a type of communication beyond camouflage; birds sing and court; whales make clicking sounds; bees dance to indicate where the food is; elephants pound the ground with their heavy feet; chimpanzees squeal and sign; and so forth. While scientists have deciphered some elements of these cryptic animal languages – and they are languages – we are still exploring the behavioral traits different animals use to communicate with each other or how they process the information. Non-human species speak in foreign tongues to us, and we can't even understand a fellow human who speaks a foreign language. We don't speak "bird" or "whale" or "dog" or "elephant" or "chimp" or "octopus" or any other animal language.

I asked Warren, my psychoanalyst friend, if he thought language was the principal distinction between humans and animals. "It makes sense," he said. "Human language is so complex and nuanced, and it allows humans to provide a wedge between what they want and what they actually do. What animal can do that?"

Although I couldn't refute his knowledge of the subtle complexities of language and the human mind, I asked him how he would interpret a panther (or other big cat) circling a prey it wanted to eat, but changed its mind and ran away when sensing some danger from another source. I suggested that what the animal sensed might be the panther's silent "language" that acted as a wedge between what it wanted (to kill the prey) and what it did (run away). Of course, this example was concocted by me on the spur of the moment, and I have no idea if such behavior would occur or if my interpretation made sense. Nevertheless, Warren nodded and said, "Hmm, yes, that's an interesting question." I wonder to what extent our fixation on the differences between species detracts our attention from the more important and interesting connections.

Consider an article by James Nestor, *A Conversation with Whales*, in the New York Times (April 16, 2016) that describes how sperm whales communicate with each other by diverse clicks. Whales live in close-knit societies, are raised by matriarchal units comprising three generations, share regional dialects and, get this, have family nicknames. A recent book, *Becoming Wild*, by Carl Safina describes in detail the human-like behavior patterns of sperm whales, which form societies obeying rules of their own "whale culture." Here's one more thing about whales to think about. Science today correlates behavior and thought with compartments in our large, complex brains that we are so proud of. Good for us. Specialized brain regions for specialized thoughts. For example, our ability for abstract thought comes from our frontal cortex in the brain.

But wait. Sperm whale brains are some six times the size of human brains and have an oversized neocortex and a profusion of highly developed neurons called spindle cells that, in humans, govern emotional suffering, compassion…and speech. The click-talk of sperm whales is gibberish and their complex whale culture is incomprehensible to us; we don't live in an aquatic environment and we're not whales. As Safina puts it, "Whales have whale culture. Elephants have elephant culture. The question isn't whether they have the kind of culture we have. The question is: What are the cultures of various species? The deeper questions: Who are we here with? What are the lifeways upon Earth?" And then in a plea for conservation of whales and other animals, he writes, "And what, really, is being lost as we wipe the wild map blank?"

Maybe if we were able to eavesdrop on a sperm whale brain…I know, unlikely, but…wouldn't it an eye-opener?

Beauty

A final word before I leave this smorgasbord of thoughts on animal brains involves the concept of beauty. If sperm whales can speak in clicks and dialects and live in orchestrated communities, and if octopus can learn from each other, is it only humans that that have an aesthetic sense of beauty? From our vantage point, a rugged landscape, the sparkle of stars in a clear sky at night, a colorful bird or insect, a graceful ballet, a concert by a virtuoso musician, a painting by Rembrandt, a passage by Shakespeare, or simply $e=mc^2$ are each beautiful in a way that defies definition. The intangible nature of beauty has long been believed to be a subjective human concept. But, does beauty have an evolutionary pathway? Do animals recognize beauty for its own sake? Could linkage to an animal brain (I can't get that thought out of my own brain) provide a glimpse to its concept of beauty?

Richard O. Prum asks in *The Evolution of Beauty* how the concept of beauty arose, and he dwells on the extraordinary ornate and colorful plumage of birds, especially the males. The oft-held view is that these remarkable – beautiful – patterns evolved because they signal robust genes and thus were selected as the fittest of the lot over time. Darwin wins again! But were colorful designs truly chosen for mating partners because they represented "good" genes – the fittest for perpetuating health and vigor and prevailing in the competition for survival? Or, do birds have some aesthetic appreciation for beauty?

Prum describes how "each lineage and species has evolved along its own distinctive and unpredictable aesthetic trajectory. The result has been the flowering of more than ten thousand coevolved repertoires of displays and desires." He reminds us that Darwin himself in *The Descent of Man* considers sexual selection among birds somewhat separate from natural selection. Although Darwin recognizes that "it is difficult to obtain direct evidence of their capacity to appreciate beauty," he writes, "... male birds display their fine plumage and other ornaments with so much care before the females, it is obviously probable that these appreciate the beauty of their suitors."

Especially intriguing is that Australian bower birds, and the Satin-bower bird in particular, collect colorful articles, including feathers, bones, shells, berries and much more, in places they congregate and display strange antics. Males are more numerous than the plain females, who inspect the various possible mates before making their choice. The decorations that males create in their spaces are highly sophisticated. If someone changes the arrangement as an experiment, the bird rearranges the décor to his taste, as an artist might. Unlike science, there's no good control. Prum believes most people would be hard pressed to claim with certainty that such behavior and distinctive – beautiful – coloration of birds only signal "good" genes for a selective advantage. Indeed, it's possible that such pleasing colors, designs and dances are a trade-off for acquiring a mate, despite compromising the safety of camouflage.

We don't know what's in the mind of any animal any more than we know what is in the minds of people we know and love. In *Becoming Wild*, Carl Safina speculates on the basis of extensive observations on birds the following:

"A taste for the beautiful exists as a deep capacity, one bequeathed to us through inconceivable ages, shared to varying degrees by many creatures. It seems to me that a sense of the beautiful exists to let living beings feel at home, happy and alive, here on Earth. If anything is more miraculous than the existence of Life, it is that Life has created for itself a sense of beauty.

"And so, behold these macaws, having such fun dangling around. Aren't they, in their splendor and playfulness, just so surpassingly *beautiful?*

"I'm sure they think so."

It's entirely possible that we humans didn't invent the concept of beauty. Keep *that* in mind when the beauty of nature, or music, or art, or anything else that next overwhelms you with its aesthetic sense. As Prum says, beauty happens.

TENNIS

Learning

I lost my first tournament tennis match 6-0, 6-0 (maybe I'm exaggerating and got a game) when I was 15 playing in the Pacific Southwest Tennis Tournament at the Los Angeles Tennis Club. As usual, Mama was watching and didn't seem phased by my ignominious defeat. "You hit some fine shots," she said. One benefit of such a humiliating loss is that it almost guaranteed improvement in the future. I couldn't do worse. I think that set my goal for life: always improve, no matter what, no matter when.

I started playing tennis at 13, which is later than for my peers in Southern California. I was given special permission to leave school to train when the last bell rang at 3:15 in lieu of participating in organized school sports. I practiced daily on school days and weekends with Tani, a professional tennis player from Romania, and played matches with other players. Over a few years I became an officially ranked junior player in the region and returned the favor to my high school of excusing me to practice tennis by winning trophies as their representative. Tennis was more than a sport for me; it was a vital part of my existence. I breathed tennis day and night. The tennis racquet felt like an extension of my arm, my callouses badges of honor. My mood soared with victories and plummeted with losses.

Really plummeted. But, in retrospect, I think there was a benefit to that discouragement: instead of slaming my racquet against the ground in a tantrum (always a temptation), I doubled my effort, almost as punishment, and stepped up a notch with each defeat. One curious observation was that almost each burst of improvement was preceded by a period that seemed like a loss of ability. That was another lesson I kept in mind as I got older: don't despair with failure, whatever the activity. Take it as a platform for improvement.

In addition to physical activity, tennis is a psychological challenge. Mumbling with self-flagellation bordering on self-hatred – "…you're so bad, such a loser, pathetic…" – is a common affliction for tennis players in the heat of battle, and almost always leads to loss. I know, often having been the loser. What a painful way to learn self-control and to bend, not break, with the wind. No matter the score in tennis, it's always possible to recover, to come back and win. Tennis exemplifies Yogi Berra's prediction, "It ain't over 'til it's over," before his team's famous comeback in baseball to win the 1973 National League pennant. There's no time limit to a tennis match, not even a specified number of innings to be played as in baseball. Tennis is about endurance, attitude and skill.

Although tennis is a competitive sport with the goal to win, it's also an art. Even if I won, I didn't want to "win ugly," as the tennis analyst Brad Gilbert called it. No two players move the same. I could recognize a colleague from a distance if I saw him or her run or hit a groundstroke or a volley or a serve. There's always a winner and a loser in competition, it's one or another. The artistry of tennis, however, lay in the details and execution: the strokes; the movement and timing; the footwork; the anticipation of where the opponent will place the next shot; the strategy adjustments as the match progresses; and the composure in the battle with oneself. In short, the artistry is the doing, not the result. It's all about expressing who you are by mastering the choices you've made.

I tried to mimic the champions at the time, to pretend I was them, to stroke the ball like they did. I imagined I was Pancho Gonzales when I served, imitating his motion, and that I was Ken Rosewall when I sliced a backhand. This may have improved my tennis, but, of course, I always remained myself; what other options did I have? I couldn't jump out of my own skin, even if I wanted to; my fantasy couldn't become reality. Tennis taught me that to emulate someone I admired didn't risk losing my own identity. How lucky is that! A prison sentence of being stuck with myself gave me the freedom to be someone else.

Timing

I was known for my mean left-handed tennis serve – power, spin, accuracy. I could whack the ball suspended above my head for a split second and make it land close to my target in my opponent's service square (okay, I missed now and then). How did I do that? I have no idea. I doubt that a pitcher could explain how to throw a baseball 100 miles per hour to cross precisely over the left or right side of home plate 90 feet away, or that a quarterback, while dodging opponents trying to tackle him, could explain how he passes a football 30 or 40 yards to reach a receiver running full speed to a designated spot on the field, or that a basketball player could teach someone a jump shot so that the ball sails between the obstructing arms of the defense and swishes through the hoop.

My best guess is that timing – an elusive sense, an internal tempo of sorts – governs that kind of skill. It's not about following a protocol. Timing is an essential ingredient when a tennis player suddenly feels "in the zone," a magical state, almost surreal, when confidence soars such that missing feels impossible. It cannot be explained to a non-tennis player who has never experienced it. The exquisite timing of playing in the zone involves…what? Seamless joining of invisible spaces between micromovements? A rhythmic dance on autopilot, the body bypassing the brain? It's certainly not the brain instructing the body. It's more than muscle memory; it's muscle judgment. The few times that I've played tennis in the zone gave me a taste of the exhilaration of creative success, that rare moment when everything converges into art.

Finishing

Finishing a tennis match that's *almost* won is an underrated difficulty. When it appears to be the opponent's last gasp, when victory is almost touchable, many factors come into play: nerves, wishful thinking, overconfidence, a pinch of arrogance, even apprehension that winning is too good to be true. It takes extra concentration to clinch victory, no matter the score. This was painfully evident in the dramatic 1993 women's Wimbledon final between the great German champion Steffi Graff and Czech challenger Yana Novotna. I was there with my mother sitting in prime seats given to us by Louise Brough, my mother's friend and sometimes tennis partner, who had won six singles and numerous doubles grand slam tennis titles between 1939 and 1979. Graff won a tight first set tiebreaker, 7- 6. Then Novotna caught fire, surprisingly crushed Graff in the second set, 6-1, and was a point away from a 5 -1 lead in the critical third set. It seemed the match was "in her pocket," as they say. Oh, no! Novotna double-faulted the serve that cost her the point necessary to win the crucial game, slid downhill thereafter, and let the Wimbledon championship slip between her fingers, losing the final and decisive third set 6-4. She cried pitifully on the Duchess of Kent's shoulder. My heart broke, along with everyone else's in the stadium. "It ain't over 'til it's over" was modified to, "It ain't won 'til it's won." The end game – victory in sight but not quite there: finishing is its own battle.

Novotna came back to win Wimbledon in 1998, how good is that! (Sadly, she died of cancer at 49.)

Resilience

The resilience needed to avoid a Novotna-like lapse under pressure can be equally dramatic and extraordinary, as I witnessed on TV of the finals of the 2015 French Open championships. Serena Williams from the United States was going for her twentieth tennis victory in the highly regarded major grand slam tennis tournaments, which include the Australian, French, Wimbledon and U.S. championships. Oh, my god: 20 major titles! I competed as a tournament tennis player in Southern California as a teenager, trained every day for years and can attest to the difficulty of winning a single tournament, even a minor, local one. Serena was seeded first, the heavy favorite against Lucie Safarova from the Czech Republic, who was seeded thirteenth and a serious underdog. In the first set Serena overpowered Safarova, winning 6-3, as expected. I felt sorry for outmatched Safarova. The beginning of the second set was even more lopsided, and quickly the score was 4-1 in favor of Serena. The match was essentially over.

Wait a minute! "It ain't over 'til it's over." This time it was Serena's turn to double-fault, and then she missed a few relatively easy shots that should have been winners. The momentum shifted. Safarova hit a stunning forehand down the line, her best weapon. Soon it was 4-4, then 5-4 in favor of Safarova.

Imagine. Another Novotna-like collapse in process, but this time by the champion.

Serena started to scream and curse, yet she kept on fighting. She recovered to 6-5 and was two points away from the championship. Close, but not victorious yet; it's not over until it's over. Safarova won the second set tiebreaker. Serena was livid.

The third set started in Safarova's favor, 2-0. Serena, her face contorted in anguish, sprayed shots wide of the mark. Safarova took control.

Serena kept pumping her fist, kept shouting in the air, but her accuracy improved. She found the lines; she retrieved her ailing serve. In my mind, I heard her say to herself, "Losing is not an option." Or was I saying that about myself?

Serena won the next six games and her third French open title; her twentieth major tournament was now history. She was smiling, a behavioral chameleon.

A Slice of Life

After the obligatory polite remarks, Safarova was stoic and respectful when she took the microphone. She promised to return and play even better next year. I heard a story about expectations and resilience, not only about winning or losing. Having extended Serena to three sets and having battled close to winning seemed a victory in itself for her, and she clutched the runner-up trophy as if she knew that. Safarova's loss to Serena was, from one point of view, a win. I recalled a tennis tournament in my teenage years when a top ranked player beat me. Nonetheless, I won a set and pushed him to a close third set. Yes, I lost, like Safarova did, but I won a set, like she did, a victory of sorts for me, which boosted my confidence and improved my tennis. Winning wasn't always not losing.

Next, Serena took the microphone for acceptance of the winner's trophy. Unexpectedly, she spoke in French with hardly an accent and said that to win the coveted French championship for the third time was a dream come true. She then switched to her native English, praised Safarova, and thanked family, friends and trainer. How many other languages did she know? What else could she do so skillfully? There was more to Serena then tennis expertise: depth and breadth, more than the performance showed.

After a brief pause, Serena said what was moving by its simplicity, "Dad, I love you so much." Her father had decided when she and her older sister Venus were children that he would make them tennis champions and predicted that Serena would reach even greater heights than Venus. This turned out to be true. But he didn't play tennis himself. Imagine. He studied it in books and created one of the greatest sports phenomena in history. There's a novel in that, I thought, the drive of vision and determination.

The extraordinary tennis, the refusal to lose, the self-conquest to prevent the match from fading away, the final victory. I wondered whether Serena's drive to beat Safarova came strictly from her competitive juices flowing at the moment. To some extent, probably. Too often I have felt the heavy pressure of competition to win. Or were larger goals going through her mind, such as putting major championship number 20 in the history books or having "the best ever" written on her tombstone? Was she living in the moment or the future? How would her life differ if Safarova had beaten her? As I watched the match progress, I was using time, evaluating who I am and who I strive to be.

Tennis became personal again, like it was years ago, more than a game, a slice of life.

LIFE, CREATIVITY AND ART

The Stream

When paging through an album of family snapshots, I reflected on my life as a chronological series of events. I saw myself at two with my face smeared with yogurt, at six on a swing pushed by my mother, at ten costumed as Superman at Halloween, at 15 on a tennis court, at 16 with my first girlfriend, at 18 graduating from high school, then college and graduate school, at 29 married, getting a dog, followed by our two sons, at thirty-something with friends at a party or with colleagues at work, all sequential notches on a measuring stick. I did this, and then I did that, and so forth. Is that a life complete, checking off a certain number of experiences in the list that society supplies? What about the non-events that lie in between the episodes?

Each recorded event is more like shrapnel from an exploding grenade. The photos are headlines, mere titles of first drafts of stories that fail to capture the feelings and conflicts of the times. A picture of my pregnant wife Lona looking happy says nothing of the excitement and anticipation, as well as the apprehension, we felt before having our first child. A picture of newly born Auran held by me ignores the wonder of seeing myself and also another human being, still a stranger, as my son. The pictures of Auran and his younger brother, Anton, celebrating their Bar Mitzvah, our Jewish heritage, is factual, but there's no trace of my not being an observant Jew or never having had a Bar Mitzvah myself. The college pictures of me smiling during my freshman year at Harvard doesn't show my fear and difficulty writing essays for the mandatory freshman writing class or my homesickness at being in Boston across the country from my family in Los Angeles for the first time. The realities of the past have faded: I remember but no longer experience the elation after winning or depression after losing a tennis match, just as I recall but do not feel the excitement of a discovery and disappointment when the experiment failed.

Yet, the pictures – the notches on the stick – *are* the frame-work of my life, despite that the memories are dimmed when seen through a different lens at a later date. I may no longer have the past sensations, but the pictures do call forth buried feelings that remain. I still often feel as an outsider, even in groups of peers, when I see my sad face in my second-grade class picture. I'm changed, of course, but I'm still the person that I was. My body has weakened, my face has wrinkled, and my scalp is now exposed (where did my hair go?), but my character did not re-invent itself.

What, then, are the criteria to select the events as the significant stepping-stones of one's life? How to distinguish the banners from the substance? Do passing moments trump the events? Perhaps, at times. Do the moments and the events fulfill the space of life? Hardly.

I propose a stream as analogous to life, with the events as islands. The majority of our lifetime is spent waiting and pre-paring for the events, rather than the events themselves. Think of the many challenges and desires – the dreams as adolescents to be loved or just liked or triumph in some way, or the ambi-tions as adults to climb the ladder of success, or the challenges as parents to readjust values along with the kids. Aren't these our lives as much as the events? I think so. That time spent yearning and working and trying are what I call the stream of life, the time backstage as it were, the true life we experience. When we reveal ourselves most meaningfully, don't we include our failed dreams and disappointments – the relationships that we let slip by or that didn't work, the opportunities we didn't take, the goals not achieved, the projects not done – as much as the events that did occur, such as, for example for me, college graduation, marriage, children, career and retirement? The grades don't represent the college experience, proposing isn't the marriage itself, promotion isn't the career, traveling isn't retirement. Remember the intervals of confusion or anxiety or procrastination. And don't forget the secrets – the unmentionable moments and humiliations – that flow within our stream, yet remain beneath, in private, for us alone.

Becoming

Less than a minute before introducing me at Christie's in New York to give a talk about my memoir, *The Speed of Dark,* Stephen Lash asked me to sum up my life in a few words. Good grief! I wasn't even able to cover my life in a memoir that took years to write. Surprisingly, however, an immediate response came in a flash: "My life has been a journey in creativity, Stephen, no matter what I did or when I did it."

He jotted something down on a crumbled piece of paper that contained a few other bits of information about me, including even that my classmate at Harvard was the infamous Unabomber (fortunately, I never met him), and then he introduced me, mentioning creativity as my life's journey. My talk went well, I covered the topics in my prepared notes – my childhood, science career, Inuit art collecting, writing – and I read the marked passages in the memoir, as planned. When I finished, I felt satisfied that I'd done what I had intended, yet the talk felt unfinished, like a superficial outline.

"Why? The talk was clear and interesting," Stephen said when we spoke later.

Yes, I thought, it would be disingenuous to say I was disappointed. Yet, I felt something important was missing in the crystallized realities. The core hadn't been expressed quite as I'd felt it. I reported accurately my childhood experiences, some of my scientific research, and what I loved about Inuit sculptures, but the realities seemed diminished, in a glass jar. When remembering that I'd told Stephen that I considered my life a journey in creativity, a process without a destination, however, I began to understand. How could anything be complete without a destination? There's always more to do, questions to answer, different perspectives to explore. Creativity is an endless parade of possibilities, it's not a goal. My friend Warren puts it as, "always becoming."

Creative expressions abound in virtually every human activity – art, literature, science – so it's not the tangible accomplishments that are incomplete, it's the relentless *feeling* of incompleteness that I can't escape. When reflecting on my memoir, I was more struck by the omissions than what I had chosen to write about, until I accepted that the memoir, whatever it covered, remained simply a book. It wasn't my life, which can't be relived in a memoir. Can any creation faithfully express the emotions and passion and doubts felt during the creative process? The experience of an event – the hopes, apprehensions, disappointments, vision, excitement, satisfaction, the moments comprising the creative process – does not exist in the final product. The product cannot be complete from the creator's viewpoint because the work is not a clone of his or her mind. As Reiner Stach describes in his biography, *Kafka: The Early Years*, Franz Kafka always spoke "of the act of writing as the truly precious element, but not of the resulting works, which always conveyed no more than a hazy image of the flash of creation (even though the author was sometimes the only one to pick up on this haze)."

Defining Moments

Coincidences often occur when the time is ripe. I found Marcel Proust's monumental autobiographical novel, *In Search of Lost Time*, while browsing in a bookstore just as I was preparing to write a memoir. I picked up *Swann's Way*, the first volume, and read snippets at random. The extended sentences comprised long strings of phrases separated by commas and folded into paragraphs. What sentences! One ran more than the page. I bought the book and later purchased the other five volumes.

I loved the descriptive prose, similes and metaphors that transformed scenes into images, like that emerging when piecing a puzzle together. I felt at times at one with the elegant salons and the empty gossip of the characters trying to impress in order not to be dropped from the prestigious inner circle. This personal connection stemmed from my Parisian visits when I was a young boy to my maternal grandparents of the Rothschild banking dynasty, who had been a part of Proust's aristocratic world. I even heard, within this deep layer of myself, my mother's voice that I act with unimpeachable decorum because I'm a Jew, as Jews stained by the Dreyfus affair in Proust's era, and must remain above reproach as a shield against anti-Semitism.

Before starting my memoir, I worried that my life hadn't been sufficiently exciting to be of general interest. My father's harrowing journey from the pogroms in pre-Bolshevik Russia to become a world-renowned cellist and my mother's brave escape from the privileged but emotionally starved childhood in the Rothschild palaces in France made fascinating stories.

Proust came to my rescue. He made what I considered his relatively uneventful life – a boyhood crush, seaside vacations, museum trips, introspective neurotic torments – momentous by filtration through his inner world. Nothing of earth-changing note actually happened. What Proust did was reflect on his precious society in terms of his private conflicts. He made writing compelling by exposing himself, turning himself inside out as it were, blending and blurring boundaries, reaching out while looking in, and having the courage to be authentic.

I thought back on my life for hints of what I might write about in my memoir. What stood out? What did I remember first? What made a lasting memory? As a scientist. I wrote about my research projects, emphasizing what I believed were the most significant findings. As interesting as these were, or at least I thought they were, they didn't represent me. Science was what I did, not who I was. It was neither the projects nor their outcomes that meant most to me when I thought about my life in science. Rather, it was my amazement when I first glimpsed the clarity and magnifying power of an eye lens – a bundled group of transparent living cells – and how the lens became almost invisible when I placed it in a Petri dish; it was the awe I felt when I watched under the dissecting microscope the beating heart propel the blood of a chicken embryo barely two days old; it was the mystery when I saw a lone jellyfish rise majestically from the depth, followed by another and then another, free, attracted to the light I beamed on the water at night by the dock in La Parguera, Puerto Rico.

What I chose to emphasize in the memoir, then, were these defining moments and other special instances etched in my mind: when Professor Leigh Hoadley kindled my curiosity when he asked the embryology class at Harvard what they predicted would happen to a frog embryo if it was cut in half; the time Alberto Monroy, a scientist I admired, told me at the Marine Biology Laboratories at Woods Hole when I was a novice graduate student that only *real* scientists would be playing hooky at the beach on such a beautiful sunny day; when my father touched my cheek backstage before turning his attention to a line of admirers waiting for his autograph after he played impromptu the Don Quixote cello concerto by Ricard Strauss at the Casal's Music Festival in Puerto Rico. What my research project was at Woods Hole, or what happens when a fertilized frog egg is cut in half, or why my father decided to switch the program at the Casal's Music Festival are all interesting – even fascinating – but the impact of the transient, special moments for me outlasted the events themselves and revealed most truthfully who I was. It's such lingering memories, not specific events, that made it all worthwhile.

Snow Magic

Snow again! Shoveling driveways, digging out cars, power outages, the misery of winter. But, I remember, there's the other side: the magic of nature.

Snowflakes, small at first, then larger, drifting downward, released from their prison in the clouds, a silence in the cacophony of life. No moving cars in the street, no people to entertain, no need for small talk. I put obligations on hold. How I love those snow days! I'll do the chores tomorrow, or the next day. How lucky to be able to say, "The next day, next week, next month." Yet, how presumptuous to take for granted that I'll have a next time. But that's how I live when the snow falls and the ground becomes white and soft. I'm in the moment then, sequestered, in a time apart from time.

Today it's snowing. I fill the bird feeder in front of the windowsill in the breakfast room. The birds have it harder than me and need food. Then, I burn logs in the fireplace and warm myself and drink hot chocolate. Lona sits beside me, which makes everything worthwhile, natural, as it should be. I sink deeply into reading *Black Wings Has My Angel* by Elliott Chaze, a short, dark novel. I've never heard of Chaze or his novel. What a gem! I believe few people know of this book, which has remained buried in literature for more than sixty years. How lucky for me to discover it when I'm buried in snow. *Black Wings* reads like a poem in prose: simple, thoughtful, a treasure. Chaze reminds me to not let life become a waiting game, as he writes: "...there aren't too many really delicious moments along the way, since most of life is spent eating and sleeping and waiting for something to happen that never does. You can figure it up for yourself, using your own life as the scoreboard. Most of living is waiting to live."

Today's snow is one of those "delicious moments" that I don't need to wait for. I'll think of snow tomorrow to remind me to make the next day another delicious moment, and then the next after that, and so on.

In Praise of Imperfections

When someone greets me with a big smile and says, "Joram, it's good to see you again," I reciprocate. "Wonderful to see you too," I might say, feigning great pleasure, although I often don't know exactly who they are. It's particularly frustrating, an imperfection with social ease as a consequence.

Although never medically diagnosed, I'm aware of having a mild case of prosopagnosia, which is the fancy name for difficulty in recognizing faces. This results in being uncertain of someone's identity when they cross my path out of context, even if I know them rather well. This difficulty is exacerbated if they had a haircut or grew a beard or were wearing a new pair of glasses. When I do *think* I recognize the person, I worry: am I right? Is she really Linda? I think so, but…or is she Harriet? I hesitate to use a name; it would be too embarrassing. What if I was wrong? So, I shake hands and wait until I receive a clue, and what a relief that is! When my wife Lona and I are together at social gatherings, she greets friends and acquaintances by saying their name out loud for my benefit. She has an uncanny ability to recognize any face of the past, no matter how many years have gone by, no matter how much they may have changed appearance.

An especially embarrassing moment came when I asked my son's new girlfriend at college what her name was after

I'd spent the previous evening at dinner speaking with her. I had no idea who she was the next morning when she was in a sweatshirt and wearing eyeglasses that she didn't use at dinner. It took me some time to live that down.

I try to look for a specific characteristic of a person's face, perhaps one eye is slightly higher than the other, or a dimple marks one cheek, however this method seldom works. There are too many people in too many places to keep it in mind and remember, at least for me. However, I will recall if a trait that deviates from the norm enough to be considered an "imperfection," for example, a stutter or strong lisp, and then, eureka! I know who it is: that imperfection becomes a silver lining of identity.

Imperfections go beyond identity marks, for we are often loved for personal characteristics that might be considered imperfections in different contexts – a defining scar, a deep bashfulness, perhaps even a case of prosopagnosia. These deviations often flag our vulnerabilities, and are commonly remembered, for we all have our imperfections, our vulnerabilities. What irony, to be identified by and appreciated for our imperfections.

The concept of imperfection depends on the man-made abstraction of "perfect" that we place on a pedestal. But perfect is unattainable because it's meaningless. We cannot achieve perfection, since it does not exist. Every science project I have finished has a caveat or two in the conclusions; every article I have published has a few errors; every tennis match I have won included missed shots, easy ones at that.

These and other imperfections are real and play, unwittingly, important roles for us. In tennis the imperfections tell me where to focus to improve. When I look carefully at design themes in a Persian village rug, I invariably find non-symmetrical, imperfect matches, raising the rug from the floor to the lofty heights of personal art, hand-made, not mass-produced by a machine. No two hand-made Persian rugs are identical; the imperfections, seldom noticed at first, help make each rug unique, add to the appeal, and give it character.

Imperfections can turn demons into angels and angels into demons. It's the tragic flaws of King Lear (arrogance, ignorance, misjudgments) and Othello (pride, gullibility, jealousy) that bring their downfall, as well as make these Shakespearean characters immortal. We remember them for their imperfection – their flaws in character. In John Kennedy Toole's *A Confederacy of Dunces*, the anti-hero Ignatius J. Reilly, a sloth, becomes an unforgettable personality due to a plethora of character flaws. Or, consider the valiant Don Quixote in his suit of shining armor vanquishing a windmill and unable to distinguish simple truth from his private ideal world, certainly an imperfection of judgment. But who can forget and not love the imperfect Don? Mozart understood the power of imperfection when he composed *Ein musikalischer Spass (A Musical Joke)*, filled with absurd sounds, wrong notes, unorthodox scales, and lopsided musical phrases to poke fun at someone or something. Imperfections carry weight and provide lasting identity.

Unintended happenings – lucky accidents I call them – might be considered cousins of imperfections and have played major roles in discoveries and scientific advances. Alexander Fleming discovered penicillin when he noted "mold juice" had killed cultured bacteria in a petri dish left accidently in the incubator when he went on vacation. Accidents have led to revolutionary discoveries and advances, such as the inventions of the microwave oven and Velcro and even the discovery of leftover radiation from the big bang origin of the universe. For me, the most important imperfection is that in the replication of our genes, our DNA. If DNA replication was perfect, never made mistakes — never had mutations by chemical misplacements — there would be no evolution, and life would be impossible.

We owe our life to imperfections.

Striving for perfection (despite the futility) to create a masterpiece, whatever the medium, is worth the effort, but the flaws, which will inevitably occur, may turn out to be the most important contributions. It's not only brilliance (although that helps), or luck (that's essential), or destiny (which is too fickle to consider seriously), but also the imperfections that mark the work.

Why Snub Good TV?

When having lunch with colleagues – all respected scientists – I brought up our pervasive world of television, especially the deluge of serials that can be streamed. As examples, I gave *Breaking Bad* and *The Wire*, both entertaining and riveting stories of the drug world.

"After a few episodes, I'm hooked. These shows may be soap operas of our era, but they're masters of sucking me in. They're genres of literature in our electronic age, quite something," I said. "Without them, I'm sure I would get more sleep!"

"Never watch them," said one of my friends. "I don't have time for TV. How do you do it?"

"Same here," said another.

"Nothing? You don't see anything on TV?" I asked.

"Well, the news."

I understand busy. I've battled overload my whole life – running a laboratory, publishing articles, lecturing, family, now writing. Yet, I'm intrigued by what we prize and snub: yes, snub.

"I go to a lot of movies," I said. "Some are good, some not so good, of course. But some are great. Ever see *The Lives of Others*?"

I got a warmer reception about movies, which were more popular than TV. But still...

"I prefer books to movies," said one of my colleagues between bites of his sandwich.

Books are prized, movies, well, sometimes, more so than the various shows on TV. Ironically, TV itself reveals the high regard of books by the general public. Many watch more TV than usual these days due to the confining lifestyle dictated by the covid-19 pandemic, resulting in a high proportion of the recordings set in the homes of the celebrities. And how do most portray the backgrounds? Bookshelves filled with books, the sign of respect and high education.

I too have high regard for books, of course, and am well aware of their strong influence and educational value. But I couldn't resist the Devil's advocate whispering in my ear. "But a lot of books are poorly written, mundane, not original," I chipped in. "You have to be selective with books as with TV or movies."

My colleagues agreed, but they said that books stimulate their imagination and participation. They were much better than movies, which catered to spectators who sit like sponges in the dark.

To some extent I agreed. Readers must construct the scenes themselves from words alone, while in movies the scenes are handed to you on a silver platter. But isn't that argument almost cliché-like? Does becoming absorbed in a movie truly exclude participation? Isn't identifying with someone in the movie involvement? I link my feelings while watching the movie with my own experiences. Someone else's story and imagination cannot rob me from my own. If that were not true, why, for example, cry or laugh while watching a movie? And here's another thought: What about the power movies have to introduce scenes you never would have imagined, something new for you, an expanded view or deeper appreciation?

Later, I wondered whether I was swayed too much by my own convictions? Was I wasting precious time by watching TV on a mindless quest for entertainment? No, I thought, perhaps defensively. Why not? Because I prize life in all its complexity, yet have lived, like all of us, only a sliver of possibilities. I never was a park ranger or lumberjack or mountain guide, but I love the wilderness; I never was a soldier or a hero of any kind; I never won (or lost) a political election or played football on a team that won the Superbowl; I never was in prison, or even had any contact with a prison, as did my son, Auran, who volunteered as a psychologist at San Quentin when he was a graduate student at Berkeley. I rely on books and movies and television, as well as friends and acquaintances, to tap these buried personalities within me, to let them breathe vicariously.

Consider *Orange is the New Black*, a TV serial of diverse women in prison who find humanity in their conflicted lives of disadvantage and crime. Is visiting that world a waste of time? Some may think so. I did at first, yet I finished watching the serial. I doubt the prison scenes were totally accurate; how would I know? But that didn't matter. Some parts were repetitious, like passages of some great books. However, even the passing video preceding each episode showing birds flying over a barbed wire fence made me confront a part of myself that, on occasion, feels imprisoned. Is that reflection a waste of time? I don't think so.

And then there's *House of Cards*, where humanity bows to ambition and pure evil. Commercially driven? Sure. No character is likeable, yet I got "hooked" to see what happens. What does that do to the myth that every story needs a likeable character to draw one in? Nonsense, I say. Maybe, probably, we all have at one time or other suppressed our chasing ambition to aim for loftier goals. Do we waste time when we visit such worlds on television?

With respect to cheering for the bad guy: Vince Gilligan, the creator of *Breaking Bad*, said in an interview that he wondered how long the audience would root for Walter White, a schoolteacher stricken with cancer trying to provide security for his family after he dies by selling drugs. White turns progressively to more and more crime that merges into evil. Interesting question. How much "bad guy" do we have in ourselves? Do we ever hurt others unwittingly by doing good? Watch some television, you might find out.

The more I accept, the more I begin to understand and appreciate, the more I think, the richer my life, and what could be safer than television and my imagination?

But, still, the major reason that I hear for not watching TV is that it's wasted time: I've so much more important work to do, or I need to develop my new hobby, or I've got so many obligations? I've already paged through *The New Yorker* checking out the cartoons or just lounged around doing nothing; I've wasted enough precious time, my most valuable commodity.

Really? Wasted time? Maybe not.

I remember eating lunch at home alone watching the TV quiz show *Who Wants to be a Millionaire?* thinking of my late father-in-law, Jack, who said when he was retired that it was his favorite program. The contestant in the quiz show was asked to decide which of four elements (sodium, lead, iron or copper) relates to the theme melody of *Batman*? Never having been a part of the *Batman* craze made it impossible for me to answer that question. In any case, it seemed like a waste of time to have such information. I waited for the contestant's response with curiosity, crossing my fingers she would know the answer, but fairly sure she wouldn't. Who would know that? Well, she said that she had watched *Batman* on TV for years as a kid, even though, no doubt, her parents must have told her repeatedly to turn the tube off and do her homework. Apparently, she preferred to waste away the time on *Batman* than do her obligatory homework. Good for her! Why? Because now, many years later, she answered without hesitation: "The chemical symbol for sodium is Na, and the theme song went something like Nah, Nah." Can you imagine?! "Yes!" said the quiz master, as surprised as I was. "Correct!" The audience burst into applause. I had that satisfied feeling reserved for success. Her answer was worth $50,000!

Finding My People

I first met Stephen Burt some thirty years ago when he was an elementary school classmate of my son, Auran. I was first exposed to Stephen's brilliance when he was in the eighth grade and visited my laboratory at the National Institutes of Health. Already then, he demonstrated a sophisticated knowledge of science. Life took him in a different direction, however, and as a tenured professor of English at Harvard, he is considered one of the most influential poetry scholars and critics today.

Stephen, married with kids, transitioned to Stephanie, an attractive and outgoing lady, whom I recently went to hear read poetry from her latest book, *Advice from the Lights: Poems*, at the Washington, D.C., bookstore, Politics and Prose. Stephanie candidly revealed her struggle for identity in her poems. Apart from the elegant expression of the internal dynamics of change from one state of being to another – the conflicts that lie at the heart of gender transitions – what struck home for me was near the end of Stephanie's talk, when she said, "Find your people."

"Find your people" recognized that we are all, like Stephanie, inhabited by more than one person. Somewhere within us different personalities compete for center stage, and the quest for identity involves understanding which of those people feels the most honest and comfortable in our skin. For me, the artist has always competed with the scientist.

Stephanie writes eloquently about searching for identity. I confess that many times poems make unexplained references that I neede to look up to be able to link ideas to images, metaphors and phrases that seem cryptic to me. But then there are those lines or short passages that sing true, even if I might be reading them in different context than the poet meant. In *Hermit Crab* Stephanie provides the image of living in another's house, and ends,

>...For a while I was
>protected by what I pretended to be.

Often, I have felt like an artist when I do science, and as a scientist when I write fiction. Am I pretending to be one or the other, or am I both at the same time?

In *Scarlet, a Betta*, using a fish metaphor, the poem concludes,

>I pretend each trace or trail
>I make in the clarified water
>amounts to my emphatic signature,
>which I have chosen to leave in invisible ink.

I have felt on numerous occasions that I've left my signature in invisible ink, a conflict of competing personalities battling it out somewhere within me. So, who are *my* people?

Stephanie recognizes the need to show that invisible ink – to expose her secret – in *After Callimachus* (a noted Greek poet, critic and scholar who lived from 305-240 BC),

Why do I write? Experience
        And scientific evidence agree:
an otherwise intolerable load
        of shame decreases by up to six percent
if told to even a temporary companion,
        through a folded-up page at recess, a performance
on classical guitar, a palinode,
        a tumblr, or a hash mark on a tree;
fears diminish, at least a little, whenever secrets
        are no longer secrets and enter the common
atmosphere, even as birdsong, even as code.

I quote this poem in its entirety because for me it relates to writing, which has acted as a foil to science and the voice transforming my invisible ink to opaque. These temporary companions, visible or invisible, are our people to whom we can reveal ourselves, transform our invisible ink to opaque. Once again, then, who are my people, the ones reading the invisible ink or the ones reading the opaque ink?

Stephanie suggests an answer in *A Covered Bridge in Littleton, New Hampshire*, where she concludes with simplicity,

The point is to be, in your own eyes, what you are.

I have found that the diverse people within me – scientist, author, art collector, husband, father and grandfather – speak with a common voice when I accept that I am simply what I am. Isn't that enough?

How, then, should I find my people? Maybe if, like Stephanie, because I'm not hiding anything or anywhere, they will find me.

Ambition

I was at lunch with friends when the subject of ambition surfaced, with a focus on succeeding. This raised the unanswerable question of, what is success?

"Well," I said, "do you mean in the context of career or family or self-satisfaction?" Thinking of my love of sports and, especially my tennis days of yore, I added, "For athletes, face it, success is winning." As the words tumbled out, however, I wasn't convinced. My friends nodded without much enthusiasm and chipped in their points of view.

"I would define success as having significant sales of my book," said the writer.

"For me, success is a tenured university position," said the professor.

"Perhaps for you," said the scientist, "but for me success means discovery."

I understood. Competitive sports weren't the same as creative activities. "The usual measure of success as a scientist, I guess, is making discoveries," I agreed, but I realized it wasn't that simple. What about an interesting discovery that was rebuked by peers? Wouldn't that be more frustrating than successful? Success needed recognition. For a scientist, success meant publications, awards and a well-supported laboratory.

Then I thought of writing, which was my present focus. I told my friends that writing a compelling book that received positive reviews matched publishing a discovery for a scientist.

"Nah, you're still defining success by recognition," the writer said.

The professor and scientist nodded. Was that really what I believed, that success always meant being recognized?

I searched my mind for a common denominator to define success in science and writing, my two creative fields, and that's when I had an epiphany.

"Success for a scientist and writer is…an invisible cannibal!" I said, testing an idea. "Success is when the idea of success submits to the work itself, when it devours itself – it's a cannibal of sorts – leaving no time to think about success."

"I don't get it," said the scientist.

"What?" questioned the writer, looking even more confused than the scientist.

The professor shook his head and remained quiet.

I tried once again. "Success is when you don't have time to worry about success," I said, excited with my new thought. "I've felt successful as a scientist when research preoccupied every moment and I was driven to follow the glimmer of light wherever it flickered. I felt successful as a writer when I was completely engrossed in trying to express ideas in words that sing."

I realized that this was no more than the cliché that success was the journey, not the destination. It's one thing to parrot a thought, however, and another to suddenly understand it.

"Get a grip. You've had your share of recognitions in one form or other, so of course you can get away taking the high road," said the scientist. The professor agreed.

I concurred as well. Modesty has little impact, much less sincerity from someone who is judged as successful by peers. But it was true: when my research lagged, I didn't feel successful as a scientist; when I was depleted of ideas, I felt a failure as a writer.

"I'm not shunning recognitions – god forbid – we all need that," I told my friends. "I'm trying to define success, you know, get away from the simple-minded idea that success requires recognition. No one can win all the time. What then?"

No one looked convinced, but it was the best I could do.

My thoughts fled back to my teenage years when I played tennis with an aging Helen Wills Moody, my mother's friend, an eight-times Wimbledon Champion between 1927 and 1938. I remembered when we talked about her historic matches.

"I thought only of where I was going to hit the next ball," she said.

"Nothing about strategy, nerves, concerns about winning or losing?" I asked.

"No," she answered. "Just where I was going to hit the next ball, to my opponent's forehand or backhand, deep or short?"

Was she telling me the whole truth? Never mind. For the great champion Helen Wills Moody, success depended on the moment, where she would place the next shot, nothing more.

Can Creativity be Taught?

Is creativity innate or can it be taught? To what extent are we driven by genetics and to what extent by the environment? How much do we need to be taught to be creative and how much can creativity be better served by avoiding boundary-restrictive rules? When I asked my friend Nancy if her artistic 9-year-old grandson was planning to go to art school, she said, "I hope not!" His drawings, especially of animals, showed maturity belying his young age and were equal to many I've seen by professional artists. But, despite his impressive talent, what caught my attention was Nancy's emphatic response of no teachers, please!

I know what she meant: give the kid a chance to develop an original voice. Students copy teachers as models rather than struggle to develop their own voice. Moreover, teachers, with good intentions, impose their voice on eager students. I was impressed when I visited a class of adult artists and saw the colors, perspectives and brush strokes of their paintings similar to the instructor's. The few who differed stood out, even if they may have been technically less accomplished (I couldn't tell).

Zdenek Kostrouch, a fellow scientist interested in literature, said he liked my early short stories, but when I mentioned that I was taking writing workshops and interested in publishing, he looked distraught. "No, no!" he said. "Publish someday, maybe, but not now. Wait until you have written at least forty stories." I have no idea why forty was his magic number, but that didn't matter. He wanted authenticity. "Develop *your* voice," he said. "Don't bend your stories to satisfy instructors or critics. Striving to satisfy the publishing market will dampen your voice, or maybe eliminate it altogether." Perhaps, I thought. But, is it necessary or even helpful to know that your voice is unique? It is what it is. Perhaps peers, historians, or critics would be the best judge. Is it even possible to recognize originality in isolation? No voice is heard from a soundproof chamber.

A common question for a creative person is when to veer off the major highway; to take Robert Frost's path "less traveled by." Isn't shunning instruction or influence altogether akin to putting your head in the sand, re-inventing the wheel unnecessarily? Sometimes, I wonder, if striving for originality isn't the road to losing one's voice, whether by oneself or while being taught. Is it necessary or helpful to hide from present knowledge – to isolate oneself – to be original? The question reminds me of a lecture by the embryologist Oscar Schotte I attended almost fifty years ago, when he said, "To make a discovery in science you need two separate ingredients: first, the data, and second, the knowledge that you've made a discovery." How could you know you've made a discovery or been original if you aren't familiar with the contributions of others?

No one has the same genes, or pitch, or intonation, or experiences, or meaning of those experiences. Even in the bland Arctic covered by a monotonous white blanket of snow, each artist portrays similar animals or scenes or myths distinctly. I remember feeling despondent when I was a graduate student and a professor at MIT published an experiment similar to mine. In science lingo, I was "scooped," my project stolen from me. Would my research now be publishable? It wasn't officially original anymore since similar work done elsewhere was published before mine. Oh, the agony and pressure of research! "Don't worry," my mentor Albert Tyler said, trying to assuage my anxiety, "You'll never be so lucky as finding the same thing or seeing it the same way in your experiments!"

Smart man.

No creative work is entirely unique; no evolution takes place without common ancestors. Japanese art influenced Van Gogh, and African art influenced Picasso, but no one considers them derivative artists without a strong voice of their own.

Each work is original if the artist is authentic. Each previous work of an artist influences his or her next piece. Teachers are a foundation for creativity, not an obstacle. Teaching and learning are inseparable, as are teachers and students, as is reading and writing. Voice is an expression, not creativity itself.

Thus, the paradox: original voices emerge both despite of and from collective efforts, from repetitions and influences, and, yes, from teachers, who I doubt can block a unique voice any more than create one.

Boredom

"I'm bored!" Chilling words that most, if not all, parents have heard raising children. What the kid really means, or what I heard as a parent, was "Entertain me!" Usually, I complied, at least I thought I should and felt irresponsible if I didn't. Wasn't it my parental responsibility to occupy my children, to guide them to become educated and resourceful, not to abandon them when they were bored? How to entertain a bored child? There's a challenge. What if it's raining, which limits outdoor activities? There's always television and its cartoons or other insipid programs weaved in between the commercials, or – help! – what about suggesting killing bad guys in videogames. Not those again! What then? I can't stand another board game. Maybe bring out the crayons and paper pads, or how about a book? But these are adult suggestions, conventional and unimaginative – borderline boring! Boring suggestions for bored kids. No wonder the kid's bored with such boring parents!

Why should I belittle myself for lack of entertaining ideas or try to be creative, when it's the kid that's bored, not me? Did I really need to stop whatever I was doing and become a playmate to an 8-year-old on demand? Why should I become bored so that my kid won't be bored?

Pamela Paul considered boredom in children in her article, *Let Children Get Bored Again*, in the New York Times (May 2, 2019). She pointed out "during the lost age of underparenting, grown-ups thought a certain amount of boredom was appropriate. And children came to appreciate their empty agendas." She made the case that "boredom spawns creativity and self-sufficiency…boredom leads to flights of fantasy…ultimately, to self-discipline. To resourcefulness." Boredom, she said, is an unavoidable part of every activity throughout life, so might as well learn to deal with it. That's an education in itself.

A bored child left alone might create imaginary characters to play a fantasy game, which might ultimately become the foundation of an original short story many years later, or who knows what else the kid will dream up? No doubt it's something that I wouldn't have imagined. Seeds for a new videogame might be planted unwittingly in the child's mind by splashing in the mud. I wouldn't have suggested it, maybe that's why the kid chose it. Wouldn't it be more interesting to ask what he or she thought about while sloshing around in the mud, and why he liked it, or didn't, rather than channel his thoughts and imagination?

Pamela Paul was right: let the kids get bored and wade in a puddle of potential creativity.

Of course, it doesn't always work. Children, as well as adults, require suggestions or active help at times. I don't advocate letting anyone stew in confusion or frustration – in short, being bored and not knowing what to do – for too long. There's a thin line between allowing imagination to roam and the increasing frustration of boredom. However, *my* idea or project can never be as exciting to the child as one he or she dreamed up. Okay, the kid figures out something to do, but it's not working. What to do? Ignore the failures, I say, especially at first. They're like mosquitoes in the summer – bothersome, but not fatal – and sometimes even helpful. Creativity cannot be administered; minimizing management can provide opportunities for creativity to flower.

Boredom can show its faceless grin no matter what. As a scientist I've often been bored making rote measurements, and as a writer I've been bored proof-reading. But when I'm bored it's also true that my mind wanders to places it seldom has time to visit, and I have been surprised how many times these thoughts have resurfaced and been beneficial. Boredom can be an opportunity to realize the mirage dancing on the horizon; boredom can be the wrapping around the package to remove to find the treasure inside.

The boredom watching seconds merge into minutes differs from the boredom of routine. On occasion, breaking the boredom of empty time by sheer force can awaken creativity and inspiration. My method is to fake it, say by beginning a story without a plot in mind, never mind if all I can think of is a first sentence that I know won't remain. Often that first sentence suggests a second, and so forth. It's 99% perspiration and 1% inspiration, as Einstein said.

Waiting for the guiding light before fumbling in the dark is usually futile. Work – breaking the stranglehold of that kind of boredom – breeds ideas and inspiration. It's alchemy: transforming the mundane to the exceptional, rearranging the old to create the new. It doesn't happen easily or always. No wonder it's so maddening and discouraging! But then again, no wonder it's creative, for it builds a structure on a foundation of air.

Pamela Paul concluded her article by saying, "…we could do with a little less excitement." I prefer to let boredom be a breeding ground for excitement. Boredom masquerades as a blank page upon which to write something new or unexpected, a blessing in disguise to be respected. Boredom is like a snow day for kids that closes school, a gift, a potential time for creativity. Sometimes I think I'm most creative when bored, my imagination unguarded, novel ideas coming and going as strangers drifting in and out of a public space, ignoring me, until I speak to one, who may respond and tell me stories I've never heard before, and suddenly I'm not bored anymore.

Looking Back to Move Ahead

The study and consideration of early scientific ideas are often left to scholars and historians. But this can sometimes make it seem that new discoveries, minor and major, sprout from the void, or are the result of one or two singular geniuses. This is seldom, if ever, the case. Moreover, such neglect makes it almost impossible to appreciate the influence of the past for new discoveries.

In *The Swerve: How the World Became Modern* by Stephen Greenblatt, the protagonist, Poggio Bracciolini, discovers a poem, *On the Nature of Things*, that had been written fifteen hundred years earlier by Titus Lucretius Carus (99 BCE – 55 BCE). The author was virtually unknown when the poem was found, and this was his only surviving work. One might think that Poggio's discovery of the author from antiquity might have become a footnote in history, but it turns out to have been much more than that. The poem's visionary ideas on the structure of matter, magnificently expressed, made it highly influential much later in history.

In his poem, Lucretius accepted the pagan Gods – he wasn't an atheist in the modern sense. He believed the Gods had no interest in humans and so there were no reasons humans should be interested in them. He denied the existence of any creator or divine providence, which he considered fantasy, and limited the human world to what humans could perceive.

But what then accounted for what was perceived? Atoms did, he said. Tiny invisible, indivisible, immutable, infinite in number and constantly moving "first things" – atoms – came together forming different shapes, split apart, came together again in different configurations, and so forth. Even vision was the result of atoms released from the objects and invisible until they struck the eye. (Today we know the invisible atoms of Lucretius's imagination are photons.) Whatever was seen, or even thought, resulted from the random collision of atoms. When they came together, it was creation, and when they split apart, it was destruction. The perceived world was dynamic: creation and destruction were always in equilibrium.

And the swerve? That was the minimal random motion of the atoms that prevented them traveling in parallel paths. Greenblatt quotes Lucretius, "At absolutely unpredictable times and places they deflect slightly from their straight course, to a degree that could be described as no more than a shift of movement."

Lucretius was not the first person in history to imagine atoms. Leucippus of Abdera preceded him in the fifth century BCE, his student Democritus adopted the idea, and Epicurus considered all observable bodies, from the sun to grains of sand, made of similar atoms. That the "atom" concept turned out to have truth and importance to contemporary science was fluke, of course, since neither Lucretius nor his predecessors had any evidence for their speculations. It was pure imagination.

Here's what I find interesting: Poggio's recovery of Lucretius's poem stirred up questions in the Renaissance about religion and the nature of things. Lucretius's imaginative ideas in his poem contributed to the intellectual foundation for innovation in science fifteen hundred years later. Lucretius's unfounded speculations – mere words on papyrus – became an indispensable part of future creativity: old roots fed new growth.

Would any discovery be recognized as a discovery without historical relevance? Would the discovery of genes as interrupted stretches of DNA sequences have had the same impact in the absence of the rich history of speculation of what a gene might be?

I felt the weight of the past as a reference for judging new findings as I was reading Darwin's *On the Origin of Species* when I was writing *Gene Sharing and Evolution* on my research on gene expression in the eye. Darwin provided compelling evidence that incremental changes drive evolution. But my team's research showed that radical changes in protein functions also played an important role in evolution. The significance of showing relatively rapid and abrupt changes driving evolution could be fully appreciated against the earlier discovery of the evolutionary importance of incremental changes.

The past provides the background and foil for innovation.

Appreciating the influence of Charles Lyell and the ideas of other geologists on transformations in the earth's crust are crucial in understanding how the evolution Darwin describes came about. The recent book *Evolution Before Darwin: Theories of the Transmutation of Species in Edinburgh, 1804 – 1834* by Bill Jenkins goes one step deeper by pointing out the radical thinkers who contemplated the topic before Darwin.

History and speculation – sometimes correct and sometimes not – contributes to and enables the recognition of creative advances. We are left with this paradox: we advance by looking back.

Crossing Borders

Although I start conversations with genuine interest, it doesn't take long until my mind wanders. I am a poor listener. I have learned to appear engaged in the conversation, even when I'm not. My mind also drifts in lectures, movies, concerts, just about everywhere! This isn't an all or none drift, however. I have gradients of not listening. Sometimes I remain partly involved, somewhat like multitasking with partial concentration on each task while thinking about something else. The drifting thoughts usually take precedence. When the conversation ends, if one can still call it a conversation, I'm often not quite sure exactly what was said. Thank goodness for my wife, Lona, who is a perceptive listener and always remembers exactly what she heard. She learns a great deal about diverse subjects by paying close attention, as well as about the other conversationalists, their interests, their lives, lots of gossip to boot. My drifting mind is a frustrating handicap, and makes me wonder, just what world do I inhabit?

I had thoughts about my private world when I attended the Bar Mitzvah of Oliver, my nephew Evan's son. I followed in English as the rabbi read Hebrew from the prayer book, and I listened with modest familiarity to the tunes sung by the cantor and congregation. I attend services of any kind with modest interest. I'm not observant and never had a Bar Mitzvah myself. My interest spiked during the ceremony when Evan, a fine cellist, went on to play *Prayer* by Ernest Bloch. I recalled my father, who had arranged the composition, and played it on the same Stradivarius cello 44 years earlier at the Bar Mitzvah of Evan's brother, Jonathan. As the music flowed from Evan's cello I entered a private world of my own, as if I'd crossed a border between two entirely separate existences: my past and the present. And that's when I had the idea of parallel universes. I imagined I lived in separate spheres, each governed by different rules, and I inhabited only one at a time.

Eureka, a creative insight! I could be both an atheist and religious, depending upon which universe I inhabited at the time. While I could cross the borders between these parallel universes, depending on the circumstances, I could only truly understand the one I was in at the moment. Nonetheless, while in one universe, the other somehow had an influence on me, a type of background effect, a partial fusion of the universes, like my mind drifting during Oliver's Bar Mitzvah.

I wondered how many parallel universes might I occupy in my life – science, art, writing – and how, if at all, these separate universes interacted? And what about the latent personalities within me who make rare appearances, or never escape my mind? Are they each living in different universes, or are they different dimensions of the same person in one universe?

Salvator Mundi

Appreciating creative art such as Leonardo's paintings for its own sake may be considered a grass roots affair: you love it, or you don't. Giving a financial value to art catapults it to another sphere quite different than purely artistic appreciation. Hierarchy through the marketplace floats in the sky. Consider the Christie's auction for *Salvator Mundi* by Leonardo Da Vinci.

"Going once...going twice...sold," said the auctioneer, as he pounded the gavel. The spectators gasped. Imagine, $450.3 million dollars – almost half a *billion* dollars.

But a Leonardo painting! That's rare and special. As Walter Isaacson emphasizes in his biography, Leonardo was an unsurpassed genius of the ages. He blended science and art with insight centuries ahead of his time in painting and engineering and anatomy and astronomy; he even compared the relative flapping speed of the wings moving up or down in different species of birds, and applied his findings, along with his anatomical studies, in attempt to engineer human flight. His extraordinary innovative paintings are treatises on light and shadows and tell stories uniting the earth and mankind. As Isaacson wrote, Leonardo was "the epitome of the universal mind, one who sought to understand all of creation, including how we fit into it."

There's a case to be made that *Salvator Mundi* – one of the few remaining paintings by Leonardo – is worth whatever someone can pay. It's beyond creative art per se; it's history. I wonder, however, if the record-breaking sale of *Salvator Mundi* delivered an ironic message with respect to our current values. Leonardo buried himself in his polymath work – painting, engineering, science, irrigation, city planning – so deeply and was so often distracted that he seldom finished anything, at least not to his satisfaction. No one could count on him.

Would Leonardo have created the works he did if he had met his deadlines? How different from today's rushed, over-committed world with constant targets to meet. I wonder what would happen today if we finished little of what we started, or made it too ambitious to be successful, as Leonardo often did, or left it incomplete to pursue another project because of our curiosity? Research grants in science that stretch the imagination or are considered overly ambitious or proposed strictly to satisfy curiosity have difficulty being funded today. They're called fishing expeditions, meaning they are too risky. We'd be out of work if we followed Leonardo's example: a scientist would lose support, a professor would be denied tenure, or a researcher would be fired from industry if his bright ideas never materialized on time.

Moreover, Leonardo never published. He did, however, keep meticulous unedited, disorganized notes – over seven thousand pages of descriptions, diagrams, lists and thoughts – his mind on paper, his curiosity on his sleeve. Compare that with today, when success in science and art and engineering, Leonardo's worlds, is measured by publications and sales and immediate usefulness.

The irony of *Salvator Mundi*, then, is that Leonardo's success, judged by Christie's mind-bending sale, reflects a creative lifestyle that has been lost in modern times.

I know, for every argument there's a counterargument, for every era, there's a new set of rules. If Leonardo had published his amazing observations and ideas, he may well have been credited with being the father of Newtonian physics, modern anatomy and astronomy, and the inventor of flight instead of having the Wright brothers given that distinction. Instead, Leonardo had the good fortune of having his copious notes preserved so that we can appreciate him retroactively. Diverse individuals and creative lifestyles in different eras are not comparable. But I can't help wondering that if Leonardo had followed the present criteria for success, would he have had time and freedom to be the artist that painted *Salvator Mundi* that sold for nearly half a billion dollars?

Ivory Crush

Conservationists cheered, no doubt with good intentions, during their wave of destruction to protect elephants and marine mammals from poachers. In Denver in 2013 and two years later in New York's Central Park nearly two tons of elephant ivory estimated to be worth about $8 million at the time were obliterated at "Ivory Crush" events. This included more than 1,667 ivory carvings. Collectors said that some of the crushed art could have been 300 to 400 years old and may have had religious significance. But forensic analysis – which remained pending at the time – suggested it was unlikely the pieces in question were over 100 years old. Oh, is that all? It seems the preference was to crush first and establish what was crushed later.

Killing elephants for ivory is tragic, of course. Killing elephants for anything is tragic, and there are laws against it, yet elephant killing continues. A big problem, I agree. I don't support the killing of elephants, or of other animals.

Crushing ivory art was meant to deter killing elephants by robbing its market value. On the surface, this reasoning might seem logical – anything made of ivory will be trashed, so why bother to make it, and by extension, why kill an elephant for ivory tusks that no one will buy? Why collect something worthless?

Really? Worthless? Are black markets not profitable? Wouldn't dwindling supplies of ivory carvings – those that survived crushing – follow the law of supply and demand and raise the price of those that remained, as well as those newly made by poachers in the black market geared to collectors willing to buy treasures that were no longer sold in galleries or auctions?

There are laws against killing animals, yet elephants continue to be killed. It wouldn't surprise me if crushing ivory art was no more effective at stopping killing of elephants or walruses for their tusks than the death penalty has been at preventing homicides or that censorship has been at stopping authors from writing on so-called taboo subjects. Does it make any sense that enforcement of present laws preserving elephants or walruses or whales, which I support, is helped by eradicating ivory or whale bone carvings from the past? Destroying magnificent scrimshaw on marine ivory made by whalers doesn't save a single walrus.

Preserving art means appreciating and recognizing history, not destroying it; preserving species means protecting their environments and welfare, not mistaking past art as the culprit.

There's irony touched with perversity in crushing ivory carvings in that the crushers and cheering onlookers probably liked and admired the art. Even the Nazi's admired and valued the art they torched in caves at the end of World War II. If not, they wouldn't have confiscated it in the first place. Hitler claimed to be an art lover, he even wanted to be an artist, as he condemned "degenerate art" of the expressionists.

Different motives don't change the damage and consequences of a common act. ISIS fighters smashed antique art in the museums in Iraq because it offended their religious beliefs. They claimed that no worshipped icon should remain. The

Cultural Revolution in China destroyed art that smacked of the past. Did that serve their ability to usher in a better future?

And now it's us – censoring and crushing past art treasures. Is it really helpful to destroy works of art to save animals? Why is art – one of our stellar achievements – so often the victim, the last to receive support and the first to be scraped in tight annual budgets. How ironic that art brings tens to hundreds of millions of dollars in public auctions and attracts long lines of viewers at major exhibitions in museums, and yet is so easily discounted.

Will we next raid museums or homes and crush whatever contains bits of ivory or whalebone? What about ebony, another endangered species? Will fingerboards of string instruments – a Stradivari cello perhaps – or woodwinds be next on the chopping block? Would burning fine, old instruments containing ebony really save trees? Isn't preserving history compatible with finding alternative materials that have some properties similar, if not superior, to ebony for making new instruments? Are we so limited in imagination that we must censor and crush to save what we cherish?

Art – the eyes and voice of creativity – has been part of human culture since the days of cave drawings. Despite that art is the last to receive support and the first to be scrapped in annual budgets, especially during economic downturns, art remains a cornerstone of civilization. It brings tens to hundreds of millions of dollars in public auctions and attracts long lines of viewers at exhibitions in museums. Let's not bury past art in ashes or ivory dust. Creative art of the past is the foundation for and no less important than that of the present.

The Hand We're Dealt

"Bitch!" said the gentleman, sipping champagne watching Tonya Harding warm up on the ice.

"I hope she takes a tumble," said the lady next to him.

"What a monster," drifted across the room in a voice I couldn't identify.

These were callous comments referring to Tonya Harding I heard at a party to watch the infamous 1994 Women's Figure Skating Olympics. Her rival – the American darling, Nancy Kerrigan, who was favored for gold – had been whacked in the kneecap in an attack that was widely blamed on Harding. It later transpired that Harding's ex-husband orchestrated the incident.

I certainly didn't approve of hammering Kerrigan's knee, but I felt uncomfortable with the "Harding bashing" and with the satisfaction others had when she was disqualified due to difficulties with her skates. Despite the injury, Kerrigan won the runner-up silver medal, a major accomplishment, although a disappointment to many, including me. I too was rooting for a graceful Kerrigan victory. Alas, it was not to be; the Russian skater, Oksana Baiul, a bundle of fluffy, doll-like energy, basked in the golden glory of the throne.

Fast forward some years to when I saw the movie, "I, Tonya" about Harding's life. The movie revealed Tonya as disturbed and poorly educated young woman whose bitter mother beat and humiliated her, while driving her mercilessly since the age of four to become a champion skater. There seemed to be some similarity with Serena and Venus Williams' father driving them to become tennis champions, but the life they were born into was far different from Tonya Harding's.

Tonya's father, who she loved, had abandoned her when she was a little girl, and later her husband beat and deceived her, and even shot her (not fatally) during a violent domestic argument. She claimed she didn't know anything about the knee whack, although that was doubtful. She did admit that she sent an anonymous letter to Nancy Kerrigan, hoping to disturb her enough psychologically to skate tentatively at the Olympics. Tonya Harding was no innocent poster ad for the Olympics.

Tonya's unfortunate circumstances didn't excuse her from injuring Nancy Kerrigan at the Olympics either physically or emotionally. Nevertheless, I still recoiled from the blanket hatred on display for her at the party. Favoring Kerrigan was understandable; she was an innocent victim and deserving of gold. But I couldn't answer convincingly why I felt apart from my friends at the party. It was neither rational nor connected with being right or wrong. It wasn't her figure skating expertise or celebrity status or life of abuse. I couldn't identify with any of those. My life was entirely different, and what else than my own experiences could I appreciate or understand enough to judge?

So, who did I judge Tonya Harding to be: a champion skater, a criminal, a liar, a tragic hybrid, a living form of Lady Macbeth or Iago, an abused person, a victim of circumstances? All of them, I think, one big package of a human being, who played the hand she was dealt. Isn't that what we all do, play the hand we're dealt?

Say "Yes"

In the short story by Dave Eggers, *Another,* the narrator is in Cairo against the advice of his government to deliver a package, which he successfully does in the opening sentence. We know nothing about who he works for or what's in the package. That's irrelevant. More to the point of the story, the narrator, now having some free time, goes sight-seeing. He rents a horse from an Egyptian guide, who takes him to visit the Red Pyramid, which requires a desert ride of some distance. The guide whips both his horse and the narrator's and they gallop off into the desert. The problem is that the narrator has never ridden a horse before, except for a slow walk once as a tourist, and he is scared to death. He miraculously manages to stay on the galloping horse by struggling to position himself as high above the saddle as possible without falling off. Performing this acrobatic stunt, he constantly moves against the natural motions of the horse and gets his butt slammed painfully against the saddle repeatedly. To make matters worse, the narrator is unimpressed by the Red Pyramids when he gets there. Yet, he agrees reluctantly to go see Bent Pyramid requiring more horseback riding. Bent Pyramid is no more inspiring than Red Pyramid. But that too is irrelevant. What matters is that the narrator has learned to move in synchrony with the galloping horse and can now keep up with the guide without pain or difficulty (clearly a fast learner!). So, he agrees to visit still another pyramid, which requires more riding, but this time he enthusiastically tells his guide, "I want to go," he wants to see *another*, as the story is entitled.

While reading this story, my mind flashed back to my own experiences when I chose to do things for the first time without any training or knowledge of what I was undertaking. The first time was a charm. I was about four years old in Elizabethtown, a small hamlet in the Adirondacks in upstate New York. I wanted desperately to know how to swim, but alas, didn't know how. I cracked a wishbone with my mother, wished that I knew how to swim, won the bigger half, and behold, the next day I jumped into the chilly Bouquet River and swam! It had nothing to do with receiving lessons, which I never had. It was all in my mind. Believing became knowing. Voila!

The next time I thought I could do whatever I wanted was less successful and, I admit, quite crazy. I had joined the track team when I was a freshman in high school. It was a small high school and consequently, not very many kids were on the team. There was a city-wide interscholastic competition coming up and the team needed a high jumper to compete in my age category. I had never high jumped before, not even once. I asked myself, how difficult could that be? Without hesitation I volunteered to be the high jumper.

I think the coach had second thoughts because he said, "Thanks, Joram. But we don't have the equipment for you to practice."

"No problem," I said. "I'll just do the best I can at the meet."

Imagine, the coach agreed!

The meet was at a large stadium, many schools were participating, and the bleachers were filled with parents and friends. I was overwhelmed and scared, but I had no choice then: the show must go on! I was given a number to pin on my shirt. Having no idea how to high jump, I studied the kids practicing. There were two techniques. The first was a type of scissor jump, feet first. The second was called a "western roll," if I remember correctly. That was head-first, a roll of the shoulders around the bar and a landing on your back. Very cool, as they say.

The competition started and I couldn't make up my mind which type of jump I should do. I remember running towards the bar, asking myself, "Head-first? Feet-first? Head-first? Feet-first?" Suddenly the bar was directly in front of me and so...I jumped. Head-first! It was a thing of unpracticed beauty, except that my feet didn't completely clear the bar. Oops! I landed on my back and the bar came crashing down on my nose. Whack! Broken nose. End of my high jumping career. I was carted off to the doctor for X-rays. Well, you can't win them all.

But you can win some. When I was in my mid-thirties on vacation with my family at White Grass Ranch in Wyoming, I volunteered to go round-up horses in the mountains at five in the morning with the cowboys. I did have some riding experience, but not much, certainly nothing like that. But it sounded so romantic, so...I don't know...exciting to become someone else for a few hours, a cowboy, a rancher, someone I only imagined.

"Yes," I said. "I'd love to come along."

Everything went fine for a while; more than fine. I was galloping in the hills and pastures at sunrise, copying everything I saw the cowboys do, yet holding on to the horn of the saddle for dear life, and struggling not to be thrown on the ground as the horse shied one way and then another avoiding holes or rocks. Then the cowboys started yelling instructions at me, such as "Don't split the herd! Cut around to the left!" I did the best I could, although I didn't know what I was doing or exactly what they wanted me to do. Split the herd? Was I doing that? I certainly didn't want to split the herd!

Luckily, I didn't fall off the horse. Apparently, I didn't split the herd, at least not too badly. I returned to our cabin at about 6:30 to find my family still in bed. And, I had an experience I'll never forget. A cowboy on the range, herding horses, galloping at sunrise, not as a tourist, but a man on a job, not just an experience, but a glimpse of being someone else.

I have had other instances of doing things without proper preparation – dangerous things in retrospect – without training of any type, for example, snorkeling in the Great Barrier Reef, scuba diving in Hawaii on a rough day with a bad back and my son no more than nine years old, but enough said. I survived them all.

My foolish choices are not the point. The narrator of Egger's story galloped into the Sahara Desert without knowing how to ride, which opened a new world to him. I became a cowboy rounding up horses for an hour and a half and tried to high jump unsuccessfully, but felt the difficulty of accomplishment, the effort it takes to even try.

There's no moral here, no advice, no confession. It's just what I did now and then, how I preferred to say "Yes" than "No," perhaps unwisely at times, but I don't regret any of the instances. I've only regretted what I didn't do, never what I did.

Our life is our choices, both large and small, sometimes even as insignificant as what we eat for dinner – what we know we like, or something new, something we've never even thought of eating, such as raw liver, or raw heart, or raw kidney of a seal, delicacies of the Inuit, which I tasted in the Arctic. Well, that may have been a mistake! At least now I know not to do it again.

I guess I've been a lucky survivor.

Niceties, Despite it All

When I joined the National Institutes of Health (NIH) in 1967, it was an open campus – come one, come all. There were lectures, a hospital, research laboratories, and concerts Sunday afternoons a few years later.

Everything changed at NIH September 11, 2001. Nine years later, after I had closed my laboratory, I went to retrieve my books and bring them home. My office at the time was on the ninth floor of Building 10, the hospital. I put the books along with some files in a duffle bag, which turned out to be very heavy, so instead of carrying it, I had to drag the bag. I put it on the curb and started to go for my car, which was parked some distance away. "What am I doing?" I asked myself, suddenly worried that a large, unidentified bag on a curb might appear threatening, a potential carrier of a bomb, big trouble. I retrieved the bag and dragged it to the car.

There was an argument for protection against random terrorism. A chain link fence imprisoned the NIH. Employees needed identification badges to enter the campus. Anyone not an employee needed to go through security as in an airport, and his or her car was given the once-over as well. Receiving ID badges required security checks, fingerprinting, filling out forms, great scrutiny. NIH fingerprinted me four or five times. I thought fingerprints were stable!

It's grown worse, not better. Think of the blood splattered in schools, churches, synagogues and other random gatherings, and policemen shooting victims because, what the heck, those guys might be dangerous, who knows? Immigrant children are ripped from parents and sent to undisclosed locations. Hate pervades like dandelions in the wind.

Wait! Not everything is despair. What about the niceties, the acts of kindness, the unexpected pleasures sprinkled throughout my life?

There was the time that I was standing in line waiting to check in for a flight in France. For some reason the line was in gridlock and not moving. I hardly noticed time slipping by since I was conversing with my colleague Joe. Finally, I arrived at the head of the line and politely greeted the agent, "Hi!" Usually I'm impatient, but not this time.

"Mr. Piatigorsky?" she said, looking at my ticket.

That was the simplest question I was ever asked. "Yes," I said.

"You've been so patient. Thank you. I'm bumping you up to first class."

Wow! Do I need to say more? A nicety.

Another time, still concerning airlines, I was crunched in economy class feeling, and apparently looking, miserable. The flight attendant motioned for me to come with her.

"You're looking so uncomfortable," she said. She took me to the first-class section and pointed to an empty seat. "Please sit here. You'll be happier."

I did. I was. Thank you. Nicety number two.

Another time I was at a science symposium in Kyoto, Japan. When walking to the conference from my hotel it started to rain, not strongly, but persistently, and I was getting wet. The rain suddenly stopped landing on me while I was waiting at a red light to cross the street. I looked up and saw an open umbrella above my head. Where did that come from? A Japanese man dressed in a business suit, his arm stretched in my direction, was holding his umbrella over me, getting wet himself.

"Thank you," I said, surprised and grateful. He remained expressionless looking straight ahead.

When the light turned green, he turned to me, bowed and walked in the other direction.

That, to me, registered as a nicety in spades, which I never forgot.

In Japan again, Lona and I were searching for a restaurant in the outskirts of Kyoto where we were going to meet some friends. It was dusk, the street names were in Japanese and there were no visible numbers on the houses. We were lost and going in circles. The few people we asked for directions spoke only Japanese. Finally, we met a local Japanese man who understood some English. We showed him the address of the restaurant written on a piece of paper.

"Follow me," he said.

We followed for some distance and a number of twists and turns. When we arrived, he bowed (we were getting used to that) and walked away. I have no idea how far he went out of his way, but this was another notch on my stick of collected niceties.

There's more.

In the late afternoon in New York, Lona and I, tired and rushed, took a cab from the Metropolitan Museum to Penn Station to catch the Amtrak train back to Washington. When we arrived at Penn Station, we grabbed our suitcases and dashed off as the cab drove away.

After the cab disappeared, Lona exclaimed, "Oh my gosh (I think she actually said shit), I forgot my purse in the cab!"

We went to a policeman in the train station. As futile as it seemed, Lona asked him for suggestions for retrieving her purse. We didn't know the cab company, the license plate, or the cab number. All we knew was that the driver was Asian.

"This is New York, lady. Are you kidding?"

So much for Lona's purse, we thought, the cell phone, wallet with some cash and, worst of all, a special necklace I had made for her with a pendent comprising a beach stone I picked up in Antarctica. Now it was my turn to say shit.

Back home, we were eating dinner, depressed by our loss, when the phone rang.

"Hello," I said.

"Were you in a cab in New York today?" he asked in broken English.

"YES!" I answered. Could this be true?

He was a cautious man, so he asked, "Where was I driving you?"

"From the Met to Penn Station," I said.

"I have your purse."

"How did you know to contact us?"

"The number was on the cell phone," he said.

Amazing! He agreed to take the purse to someone we knew in New York (where we had arranged a generous reward for him), who mailed it back to us. We received the purse a couple of days later. Nothing gone – not a penny – including the necklace.

I guess the policeman was right in a way: it was New York, but the nice side. I concluded that most people are honest, and the world can be a happy, reassuring place, sometimes.

Recreating

Much is made of an artist's voice that speaks with distinct recognizable qualities, a unique voice that defines the creative authenticity of a painting or sculpture.

But what about performance art, an ephemeral and momentary thing that disappears with the act itself? Is the performance artist a messenger or the message? The actor transforms into a different person invented by the writer and director, one who can make an audience laugh or cry. A musician transforms the notes of the composer and makes an instrument sing like an angel. Is the actor or musician creative in the same way as other artists?

I remember asking my cellist father what he thought about this when he played the same pieces repeatedly. Did he get bored? Did he think he was creative?

"No matter how many times I play a composition, it's never exactly the same," he said. "I would be surprised if the composer thought it was precisely the piece he wrote."

"But someone else composed the music," I insisted, with a touch of unintended arrogance.

"True, yet the performer recreates, and with each recreation, the same composition sounds a little different, and it's always personal. The music is mine if I'm the performer, and then it belongs to the audience for the moment. How I play it – how I recreate the music – is creative. The composer may indicate 'pianissimo', but how soft, or 'allegro', but how fast? I may add a pause to satisfy my own creative view of the piece."

"I understand," I said. "Every recreative performer and performance has an original, creative voice."

Okay, I thought. No two actors or musicians will give the same performance. An actor in the role of a different person creates a unique person; a musician playing a piece of music is composing that music as it's being performed. It's about creative transformation. In a sense, I said to myself, the messenger is the message.

Then I thought of my research, and how I worked on the same scientific problem for years and gave similar lectures using the same illustrations repeatedly, as well as new ones, of course. Each time I saw something different in the story, or even retelling it felt different, depending on the audience, who often asked different questions that had the power to modify my interpretation of direction of the work. With each small addition, deletion or modification, I felt like an artist modifying the painting or the shape of the sculpture. And as every scientist is distinct by having a certain voice, so was I never the same person, even giving similar lectures.

Aging

Among my pet peeves is the commonly accepted notion that creativity slips away with age. What pressure that puts on the first half of life! Imagine being forty, still young in today's world. Are we really in the eighth inning – okay, the seventh – of an imaginary baseball game as we hover in middle age?

There is a contradiction in what we expect about creativity and aging. Take science, an area especially vulnerable to the idea that creativity diminishes with age. Since there is so much to learn, students don't finish graduate school until their late twenties, if they're lucky, and then they are under the direction of a mentor as a postdoctoral fellow for a number of years. Next come the years of struggling for a grant, setting up a laboratory and networking at conferences to navigate in a competitive professional world. Time flows by. Forty is almost there, or maybe it has come and gone already. We receive the conflicting message that we are to be both a student guided by a mentor during the creative years, while at the same time it is intimated we are getting on in years and are losing the vital spark of our creativity.

Yet, let's face it: social pressure compounds the idea that creativity diminishes as physical vulnerability increases with age. How many times have we heard from a person of sixty or so, or even fifty-something with a prestigious position of responsibility, "Oh, I'm not thinking about myself. It's the younger generation I'm concerned with."

How noble! How selfless!

Don't misunderstand me: I'm neither against helping the younger (or older) generation if I can. I'm just not ready to wave the white flag on my own creativity as a scheduled event.

In a recent article in *The Atlantic* (July 2019), Arthur Brooks thinks differently. He writes that he overheard an elderly man complain to his wife that no one needs him anymore and he wished he were dead! What? Dead? Brooks recognized the man as a world-famous celebrity in his mid-eighties with many past accomplishments. What was going on?

To satisfy his curiosity, Brooks started researching studies on the degree of happiness – satisfaction – with age in successful professionals. Dean Keith Simonton, an expert on trajectories of creative careers, found that productivity increased the first 20 years and started declining thereafter. That meant, start your career at 30 and prepare for decline after 50, or somewhere around these dates. I'm in deep trouble. I continued doing science research until I was 69 and then stepped into a writing career. I'm writing at 80 and still ambitious, or at least hopeful.

Brooks does give some careers a bit more time before the big decline. Professors, teachers, historians – careers that depend on accumulated knowledge rather than creativity – are considered exceptions because they use "crystallized intelligence," namely the ability use knowledge gained in the past. They don't require "liquid intelligence," the ability to reason, analyze and solve novel problems. Does that mean professors and historians don't need to reason or solve problems? They might be able to keep going until sixty or so, and maybe even older for the lucky ones. Brooks says that the biggest mistake successful people make is to try to sustain their peak accomplishment indefinitely, which he views as trying to exploit liquid intelligence as it begins to fade already relatively early in life.

I opt to give life, not an arbitrary age, the choice when to begin the ominous decline. For example, my friend Win, an eminently successful scientist since his youth, is 95, still with great accomplishment and clarity of thought.

Pagan Kennedy's article, *To Be a Genius, Think Like a 94-Year-Old*, in the New York Times (April 7, 2017) gives examples of old guys being creative, and highlights John Goodenough, who is still inventing better batteries at that age. He says, "I'm old enough to know you can't close your mind to new ideas." John Goodenough also said, "You have to draw on a fair amount of experience in order to be able to put ideas together." Where might that experience come from? The older I am, the more experiences I've had. Everything new is the same age when experienced, as a fine wine. Doesn't it take the maturity of years to even recognize what's new?

A major plus for an aging person, an aging person to be creative, to be creative is having more of what a young person needs, but seldom gets: leisure time to think and fail and try again. Time doesn't disappear until you die; for the lucky ones at least, and with age, time becomes more accessible, less clogged with responsibilities.

Years ago, my father told me that Igor Stravinsky had said, "I'm so busy, I don't have time to rush." In his book, *The Eighth Day of Creation: Makers of the Revolution in Biology*, Horace Freeland Judson quotes the Nobel Laureate James Watson as saying: "It's necessary to be slightly underemployed if you are to do something significant." David Leonhardt's article, *You're Too Busy. You Need a 'Shultz Hour*, in the New York Times (April 18, 2017) quotes the psychologist, Amos Tversky, who voiced a variation of the sentiment: "The secret to doing good research is always to be a little underemployed." The 'Shultz Hour' is an hour of contemplation and solitude, free from distractions and interruptions, closed off to the world, that George Shultz, secretary of state in the 1980s, took each week. Older people don't need to wait a week for contemplation and creative thoughts. They're underemployed, lucky guys!

Take a peek at history: think of the sculptor Michelangelo or string instrument-maker Stradivarius, who made important advances at an older age. What a shame for us if we had lost their genius prematurely.

And then there was my creative mother who believed that if you're not growing, you're dying. In an essay that is now available online, *Growing as We Age*, she wrote, "On our way to the end we may enter a transition period, as we have lost only partly the feeling of infinity. We not only know the end is close, we feel it. But we do not face it head on as the date is not set...Twilight brightens, maybe enough to permit another step, a step forward, another surge of growth. Yes, keep growing, be lucky, grow until the end."

Yes, I like that: aging as a platform for growth.

Be creative, if that's your bent, at any age.

FAMILY

Father's Day

At breakfast on Sunday morning, June 11, a few years ago my wife Lona wished me, with a touching card, a Happy Father's Day. That evening we went out for a romantic dinner together to celebrate. I was surprised how easy it was to get a reservation at a restaurant, and then how many empty tables there were on Father's Day. The reason became clear when our son Anton, to whom we had sent a Happy Father's Day email earlier that day, thanked us, wished me the same, but said we were a week early: Father's Day was the following Sunday, June 18.

I guessed we were getting old and couldn't keep straight what day it was. But then I thought, what could be more special than celebrating Father's Day on our own special day, not dictated by commerce, when "Happy Father's Day" wouldn't be more meaningful than "Have a good day," which has become a meaningless phrase said like a robot. And for that matter, "I love you," or the abbreviated "Love ya," becomes no more than a reflex for saying "Goodbye for now." "I love you" is the most powerful, meaningful expression I can think of when said at the right time to the right person. Why waste it as a rote obligatory ending to every casual exchange? Isn't it assumed among family members that love binds them together? The love is in the acts, the life together, the caring.

Sorry, I'm being a curmudgeon.

The fact is, I loved having my special Father's Day. It was mine alone. I rationalized: it makes sense for me to have two Father's Day, because that way I can celebrate my incredible luck of having two wonderful sons by making a special, separate Father's Day for each. Then, I remembered the obvious: I wouldn't be able to celebrate Father's Day at all if it weren't for Lona, the mother of my children. So, the real Father's Day should be on Mother's Day (and vice-versa for Mother's Day, of course).

It's all so confusing, until I thought of Inuit art, where parent-child, and families in general, are a dominant theme. The family nucleus is essential in the Arctic, where mere survival is so challenging. The strong bond between parent and child doesn't need a day set aside to be remembered or appreciated and expressed in numerous Inuit sculptures that I see every day.

And so, it's Father's Day every day for me, and I feel grateful to my family for giving me that gift.

The Ring

I'm still trying to figure it out. At about 5:30 in the morning Lona and I were in Suburban Hospital; at 7:30 she was scheduled for hip replacement surgery. She gave me her watch and wedding ring of 48 years to hold until she came home after surgery. I placed both in an envelope, sealed it and put it in my pocket for safety.

Midway through Lona's surgery, I reached in my pocket for some change and felt the watch, which somehow had come out of the envelope. How did that happen? The envelope seemed still sealed, although that might have happened when I removed it from my pocket? Seemed unlikely. I ripped it open to find the ring, but it wasn't there. How in the world...? I turned my pocket inside out, searched every possible place in that pocket and in every other pocket, and my backpack, but no ring.

I searched the waiting room. No ring.

"What are you looking for?' asked a gentleman.

"My wife's wedding ring. It disappeared."

He offered to help me look. "Two sets of eyes are better than one," he said.

I appreciated the offer, but where to look?

The lady in charge of the waiting room, Marga Estes, seemed concerned.

"You must have put it in a different envelope," she said.

"Impossible. I asked the lady at the registration desk for an envelope and sealed the watch and ring in it then."

Marga looked unconvinced.

"Nevertheless," she persisted, "go look."

I went downstairs, asked the same lady who gave me the envelope if she had seen the ring, which she hadn't, and then I went to the area where Lona and I waited downstairs for a short while right after she gave me her watch and ring.

No ring.

A lady was vacuuming the floor, and I thought maybe she sucked it up. "No," she said. "I didn't go there yet."

I had a cup of coffee and muffin at a small refreshment stand when Lona went to the operating room, so I checked there if anyone had seen a ring.

No.

I rifled through the trash where dirty cups and soiled napkins were thrown away. I recognized my cup since I had stuffed my napkin and muffin wrapper in it. No ring.

I reported a missing ring to the hospital security. They said they would look out for it.

When I returned to the operating waiting room, several people asked me whether I had found the ring.

"No. I can't figure it out," I said. "I know I put it in the envelope, sealed it and put it in my pocket. It can't be magic."

Apart from the frustration, my mind started drifting. Could this be a bad omen? Would Lona's surgery have problems? Would she be okay?

"Relax," I told myself. The ring has got to turn up somewhere. Yet...

"Don't worry," Marga Estes said. "Things happen. It will be all right."

Sure, I thought, but this was Lona's wedding ring.

About ten minutes went by and Marga came back to me. "I'm a very religious person," she said, "and I prayed the ring would turn up."

I was touched. She really cared. Then she showed me a thin ring. "Is this it?"

Oh my god. Yes!!

"Where did you find it?"

"Under this chair," she said, pointing to a chair not far from where Lona and I were sitting. At that time the ring was in the sealed envelope in my pocket, and I hadn't removed it.

My fellow waiting room colleagues cheered. It was time to rejoice. The ring was back!

I'll never know how the watch and ring escaped the envelope, and then how the ring worked its way under a chair nearby. Maybe Houdini's ghost was in the waiting room.

And then I started thinking of all the things that happen to us in a lifetime that we can't explain, and then forget about. It's overwhelming, really. I'm not religious like Marga is, but I'm grateful to her, and to everyone else who finds a way to keep perspective and accept help when it's needed.

We're not alone.

Fifty!

Fifty years ago – 50! – Lona and I were married on August 24, 1969 at 2 pm in Washington DC at the Hotel America. We met for the first time on a blind date (no, we both had good vision) on the day of Super Bowl 3, when the underdog New York Jets beat the Baltimore Colts 16 – 7 on January 12, 1969. We opted for coffee at the Old Angler's Inn, which we sipped slowly next to the fireplace rather than watching the game. We weren't into football until our two sons, not even a thought then, were in school. I hadn't even seriously considered proposing until the second date a week or so later. I thought it was irresponsible to make such a momentous decision on the first date. Coward that I can be at times, it took a couple of months to gather the courage to pop the question. That was just a few weeks before July 20, when we (not literally) landed on the moon, and the very day that our golden retriever called "Dusty" (for Lunar Dust) was born. Dusty, our first child, so to speak, gave us 11 puppies, delivered skillfully by Lona, but that's another story.

"Congratulations!" That's what everybody said when I told them I was celebrating my fiftieth wedding anniversary.

"Thanks," I replied. "Finally, we reached the halfway point; 50 years more to go."

Although a writer now, I must still be a scientist down deep, since I framed my response (in jest, of course) in terms of a "half-life," which is the amount of time that it takes for 50% of a group of unstable atoms to decay. I know, that's a ridiculous measure of time for a wedding anniversary, but it did make me think of the relative nature of time. The half-life of carbon-14 – 5,730 years – is used to date ancient things. I have no illusions that this measure is relevant for our marriage. The half-lives of other unstable atoms range from fractions of seconds – also not relevant – to virtually longer than the four to five billion years since the 'Big Bang' birth of the universe. Let's face it: we humans live in a tiny window of time.

So, how to celebrate number 50 – a big party, an anniversary elopement to a tropical island, a quiet evening together at a favorite restaurant? No. The choice was simple: be with our two boys (Auran and Anton), their wonderful wives (Tonje and Ava), and our beloved grandchildren (Sivan, Dalia, Klara, Reuben and Tobias), however we can accomplish that feat. Assembling all 11 under one roof can be like herding cats (note: I have nothing against cats).

For the anniversary day itself – August 24 – our granddaughter, Klara, 15, came for a short week from San Francisco to visit us in Bethesda. Lucky us! We had that quiet dinner at a special restaurant with her. Nothing like a beautiful granddaughter to appreciate the wonders of 50 years of marriage.

Then came the extravaganza. We arranged for the whole family (except, unfortunately, Sivan, our 20-year-old granddaughter, couldn't join us since she had just started her senior year at Wesleyan College) to meet over Labor Day weekend at Mohonk, a resort in the Catskill mountains not far from New York. The numerous activities there – hiking, swimming in the lake or pool, *eating*, boating, square dancing, *eating*, reading, massages, *eating*, yoga, carriage rides, and then more, before a final *snack* – gave everyone, from 12-year-old Tobias, Auran and Tonje's son, to 79-year-old me, and everyone else in between, the choice and freedom to do as they would like. That's a find! And the resort was 150 years old, which made me feel young.

Now, here's the conflict for Lona and me: do we accumulate activity points or chill out with a good book (and ice cream on the side) while the young guys are running around?

"Auran, did you swim across the lake?" I asked.

"Yeah. About 25 times." He said it all as a matter of routine.

Twenty-five times!!! Actually, he admitted that he exaggerated a bit. Oh, and his wife Tonje swam with him. Are they kidding? I would need to take my cell phone to call 911 at the midway point of the first crossing. Well, I had to keep reminding myself that this was my 50th anniversary, and can say, "Been there, done that. Give me a break!"

"Hey," I asked Anton, who was with his daughter Dalia, 16, and son Reuben, 13, "what are you guys planning to do this afternoon? It's a beautiful day?"

"We're going to climb the lemon squeeze."

"What's that?" I asked.

"It's rock climbing over boulders and ladders and scaling the rock wall within a tiny crevasse, apparently only a fraction wider than our bodies."

"That sounds like fun," I said, with a certain apprehension. "Maybe I'll come with you."

Silence. "Maybe that's not such a good idea, Dad. It's pretty rugged."

Lona was too intelligent to even suggest going. And, of course, my threat of accompanying them was not serious. I'm not out of my mind yet. It was hard enough to remind myself this was my 50th anniversary, but having my kids remind me?

That was another matter! By the way, the whole family (minus the grandparents!) climbed the lemon squeeze, and pictures confirmed Anton's point; it was rugged. They were happy to survive, but it was terrifying for some. Lona and I went on a peaceful, beautiful hike to where they emerged from the lemon squeeze.

Aging can be a privilege.

Never mind. There's more to life than rock climbing. Lona and I square-danced after dinner once. How's that for plunging into physical activity with kids 10 and younger as well as with adults. Don't laugh. I was sweating at the end.

The carriage ride to magnificent views with Lona, Auran and Anton and the four grandkids, pulled by two mules that looked just like horses, was great. Somehow, I always thought that mules looked like donkeys, but that doesn't seem to be always true. Live and learn, even on my 50th.

Then came our anniversary dinner. We all dressed up fancy and had our mandatory group picture. It warmed my heart with love and pride to see the two of us – Lona and me – having produced such a special, good-looking bright family. It made me think of my father and pregnant mother (with me) and two-year-old sister, Jephta, who came to America in 1939 to escape the war from France. I was born six months later in Elizabethtown in the Adirondacks close to Mohonk. Thus, my immediate family grew from 4 in my childhood to 25 before my parents died, and then, sadly, Jephta succumbed to Parkinson's earlier this year. But with all our grandchildren, plus five nephews from my sister, our family will keep ballooning. I'm looking forward to our 100th anniversary!

We ate (again!), toasted, talked, laughed – especially after dinner and bloated with wine – and, well, and nothing. We were together, the ten of us, on our 50th wedding anniversary. That was more than enough.

DEATH

First Tastes

"Roosevelt just died," said my mother on April 12, 1945, with tears in her eyes. I was standing in the aisle next to our family compartment on a train looking at the passing scenery. That's when I had my first contact with death. I'd never heard of President Roosevelt – FDR. Five-year-old kids don't worry about politics. But I remember sensing that his death was a big deal, stamping death in my mind as an irreplaceable loss.

My second exposure to death occurred four years later when my mother received a telegram on June 30, 1949, saying that her father, Baron Edouard de Rothschild, had died in Paris. He was 81. We had just moved from Philadelphia, where my father taught cello at the Curtis Institute of Music, to Los Angeles, in response to my pediatrician's advice that the milder Southern California climate would benefit my recurring earaches. Grandpapa, who I hear in my mind with a French accent, had spent time at a sanitorium to treat tuberculosis many years before I was born, and I don't think that he ever recovered completely. Whether true or not, I saw little of him when I visited my grandparents in Paris the summers after the war. He was not well, spent most of the time in his bedroom and didn't have meals with us. Although his death didn't feel like a personal loss to me, it was a distant warning, more intellectual than emotional, that death strikes family members.

I had a more direct experience with death in the 8th grade one morning when I arrived at my school (Black-Foxe Military Academy). The headmaster, Major Harry Gaver, had died suddenly overnight. Really? Major Gaver? Our headmaster? I had seen him in the hall the previous day, and now he was dead? Death switched suddenly from an abstraction to reality, although it still hadn't translated to my own vulnerability. In contrast to Roosevelt's and Grandpapa's death, Major Gaver's death raised questions that included personal consequences. Who would become the new headmaster? How would that affect me?

Death struck even closer to home when I was 15. Herman Steiner, the former American chess champion and Mama's chess mentor, as well as the father of my best friend Eugene, died unexpectedly from a heart attack at 50. What a shock! Disbelief ruled the day. I remember trying to console Eugene, although I was struggling to grasp the finality of death myself. Eugene's father was there one day and gone the next, never to return. Never. Yet, I still didn't feel *my* vulnerability, that death would target me someday, that my life toed a razor-thin line that I would have to cross in the future.

Death was still for adults: presidents, headmasters, grandparents and even parents, though parents' demise was more difficult to swallow. Death was impressive, but still not threatening to me. I was alive and my immediate family healthy.

Thief

A more frightening and upsetting experience occurred when I was a young teenager. Near bedtime my mother, exhausted from a hard tennis match that day, complained that her ankles felt swollen and her chest hurt. She must have considered these unpleasant symptoms as precursors to a heart attack. Looking worried, she handed me a piece of paper with the combination of the old, clunky safe in her bedroom. "You should have this in case I should die tonight," she said, just like that. I remember her tired-looking face at the time.

Was she serious? Die? My mother? What's going on? To this day I can't believe that she said that to me. At that moment, death became personally threatening – not that it would cut *my* life short, but it would leave me motherless. Since my father traveled extensively, my mother's death would have left me "almost" an orphan. That's when I learned about the stealth of death, how it's a thief that leaves others behind, and I would have been the abandoned one.

Bewildering Democracy

I cannot fathom my own death. It bewilders me. I can't mimic death in any way. My Last Will and Testament feels like a work of fiction. Even when asleep in a suspended state between conscious and unconscious, I dream and then wake up. More important, I know I'll wake up, or is that an assumption? One day I may not. Although I muddle in a puddle of thoughts about my inevitable death. I cannot avoid feeling deep roots anchoring me to life forever. I'm mortal, feeling immortal. I experience pain and pleasure with intensity and cannot imagine not existing.

Oh, death! The certainty of disappearing.

Sometimes death kills slowly, as Parkinson's disease strangled my sister, Jephta, at 81, or as lung cancer consumed my father at 73. Sometimes creeping age wins the battle, as it did to my father-in-law, Jack, at 96, and my mother-in-law, Ida, at 103, and my mother at 100. Sometimes death's victory remains mysterious, as for our fetal son in utero and for our trisomic-13 son just six hours after birth, and for Anton's father-in-law, Stephen, 67, who went from apparent health to death by organ failure within two weeks.

Death always wins, with its infinite tricks and limitless weapons. It takes no prisoners, as they say, and makes no distinction between king and serf or wealth and poverty. In that sense, it's truly democratic.

Frici

In the case of my close friend and scientific colleague Frici, death struck suddenly, unexpectedly, dispassionately.

I was home ready for bed when my colleague Joe Horwitz called me from Kona, Hawaii, where he and Frici – Frederick Bettelheim, a vibrant, 80-year-old Hungarian biophysicist who was a close friend of ours – were attending a science conference.

"Joram, I have bad news," Joe said in a somber voice. "It's Frici."

"What happened?" I waited for Joe to fill me in.

"Frici gave his talk in the morning, had lunch and went out to play tennis in a good mood."

That sounded like Frici.

"And then he fell on the tennis court," Joe continued.

That didn't seem so terrible. "Is he badly hurt?" I asked.

Joe paused. "He's dead."

What? Frici dead? He had survived anti-Semitism in Hungary and then the Nazis. After the war he forged documents to help Jews immigrate to British-occupied Palestine and was wounded as a member of the Israel Defense in the war for independence. He immigrated to the United States, earned a doctorate in biophysics and became the chairperson of the Chemistry Department at Adelphi University in New York.

After retiring, he continued his research at National Eye Institute down the hall from my laboratory.

"Dead?" I asked, hearing my words as coming from outside my body.

"Heart attack, I suppose," said Joe. "Maybe a stroke. He fell to his knees and his tennis partner heard, "Oh, my god," or something of the sort. Then Frici fell over...dead. It was immediate."

"Would you call Adriel" Joe asked, reluctantly. Adriel was Frici's only child and a journalist who had spent a summer in my laboratory as a student intern.

"Anything to help," I said, not relishing that idea.

Telling Adriel broke both our hearts.

Frici was sixteen years older than me. Lona and I accompanied him once to his childhood home in Gyor, Hungary, and he showed us the corner apartment where he had his Bar Mitzvah party. We were with him in the run-down Jewish temple in Gyor he had attended before the war when he first saw his mother's name on the list of Nazi victims in concentration camps.

Having lived through the worst of times, Frici tempered my occasional outbursts against right wing politics.

"You have no idea what Fascism is like," he'd say. "The United States is a free country. No one is going to knock on your door and drag you off to prison because you're a Jew."

Frici had lived through tyranny and wars only to die on a tennis court in peacetime. How unfair! How insensitive death can be! After a difficult divorce and finally in a golden period after a lifetime of survival and work, Frici rediscovered and married his childhood sweetheart, Vera. He was a respected professor with a fistful of scientific accomplishments and loved by his family and friends, including me. And then death clobbered him, with disregard, as squashing an ant.

Perhaps Frici had just stroked a fine forehand drive having struck the sweet spot of his tennis racquet when he dropped to his knees submitting to death's command. No doubt the sun was shining in the blue Hawaiian sky, possibly with scattered white, cumulus clouds, and the humid heat relieved by a pleasant sea breeze: a perfect day. Death ignores the weather as it does everything else. For death, weather, time and place float in space. How to find "everywhere" or "somewhere" or "nowhere" on the map?

Death substitutes *nothing* for *everything*, and *nowhere* for *everywhere*.

Death struck Frici with uncanny precision like a sniper, not like a bomb reduces a building to rubbish. There were no damaged fragments left, only lifeless meat on bones. He had no ambition or love or hatred remaining in the wake of his death. Frici's tennis match wasn't finished when he died; it simply ceased to exist, like the rest of him. Whoof! It takes a magician to go from *everything* to *nothing* in one step. But with death it's not magic; it's real and unimaginable.

Void

My friend Warren told me that he considered his experience of being under anesthesia as what death would be like. "It felt like a discontinuity that leaves no memory or other trace. No pain, no feeling, nothing," he said, dwelling on the "nothing" as a simulated death. The difference was, of course, that he woke up and could, paradoxically, describe the lack of feeling – the "nothing." But was that "nothing" anything like the void of death? I think of Warren's anesthesia as analogous to halftime at a football game, a scheduled break in the action. Brain waves persist under anesthesia. What type of hidden consciousness do they serve?

Anesthesia has nothing to do with the void of death. An anesthetized brain does not lose its stored information; it's not a dead brain. Warren remembered what preceded anesthesia, and he clicked back into gear upon awakening, even if he felt a strange inability – a frustrating discomfort – to grasp his feeling of "nothing" when he was anesthetized. Perhaps he had forgotten what he had felt under anesthesia. There are anesthetics that make it impossible to remember what happened to you. Who hasn't occasionally been unable to recall, or denied recalling even without having been anesthetized, what had happened or been felt in the past? What about *déjà vu*, such as the famous shell-shaped Madeleine cookie, that inspired Marcel Proust's flood of memories recalling the buried past in his novel, *Remembrance of Things Past*.

Negative evidence – not recalling – is never conclusive, as scientists know so well. Positive evidence – what is recalled – means more, although that can be mistaken. Memories are famously flawed. Think of the unfortunates imprisoned due to mistaken identification by a witness who "remembered" falsely what the victim looked like. Too many times we remember and forget what we'd like to, what is consistent with our incomplete knowledge, rather than what actually existed.

When dead, nothing's left to remember or forget in the void.

Legacy

How might I prepare for my own deadly disappearing act? Perhaps by legacy. Although death obliterates everything learned and felt and thought, it cannot steal what's left behind. This gives me a chance to live in absentia beyond my death, to have my descendants know something about me, at least a small morsel to brag about. But why care about legacy, an ephemeral figment of an abstract future, invisible as air? Legacy seems futile, a death-defying notion with which to hitch a ride on the coattails of those left behind or yet to come. What a strange, almost perverted, idea to make death my savior, or push me from the present to an imaginary future.

"What nonsense," said a friend. "I live in the present. What happens when I'm gone is of no concern to me."

Legacy may be considered an antidote to death, at least for some. Think of the dead of the past: Plato, Shakespeare, Beethoven, Einstein, Picasso. I could fill a book with names of such creative icons that live on through their legacy. Are they truly gone? Yes, of course, they're dead – caput – and yet no, they continue to appear in one form or other in our lives. Beethoven's compositions, or the wonder of blind and deaf Helen Keller, or Shakespeare's plays. I know, it's history, not the person who created it, but still....

History? Well, there's a conundrum. History is commonly placed in the past, but it's in the present too, and affects the future. William Faulkner wrote in *Requiem for a Nun*, "The past is never dead, it's not even past." So, there you are, a paradox for sure: you cannot fully die if the past is never dead. Legacy lives on.

Postponement

Death kills who we are and who we might have been. It swallows our realities and dreams. And so, we postpone death the best we can – eat foods that are good for us, exercise, act cautiously – striving for longevity in a valiant effort to remain healthy and engaged in our privileged life. Our concern, for good reason, is our bodies, what we see and feel – we want to keep our bodies alive and well. I am no exception. I want to exploit life to the fullest and postpone the conversion of my body to a corpse.

But I am larger than the single beast of flesh and blood. Within my mind are other personalities – some extroverts, some introverts, some ambitious, some adventuresome, others less so. These undeveloped souls – ghosts that wander in my mind – also beg for life to fulfill far-fetched dreams. These diverse souls will die with us; we don't die alone, but with our many selves. Postpone their death as well. They must not be sacrificed unwittingly by neglect or fear in our cautious quest for longevity. They are vital parts of who we are, invisible but there, and can take us to foreign territories, extraordinary places that may exceed our imagination, if we let them breathe the air our bodies breathe. At 50, I gave life to my artist personality by collecting Inuit sculptures, and then, 20 years later, I freed my writer personality. How exhilarating to recreate myself, to release my other selves, to postpone their death.

Partial deaths exist as well. One form I call (facetiously) "premature death" – an anticipatory death, a preparation death, a death before death. A premature death can obviate future difficulties due to ailing health, as well as ease the load for the executors of the estate when death arrives. I don't deny the wisdom of arranging for burial or cremation or to live more modestly – dispense with costly upkeep, sell the house and move into a retirement home, reduce possessions, simplify – trim down to coffin size. But, *when* should this be done? That's the nagging question. If too soon, might it undercut life's fullness before its time?

Warren told me, "Be careful, for how you see the world is how it is." I might paraphrase this to, "Beware, for how you see yourself is how you are."

Barring illness or incapacity, I want to see the world in full color and postpone the shades of gray as much as possible. Why place passion on the side or throw ambition out the door? Why invoke a type of living death, a premature death? What's the rush?

When I'm asked, "Why did you start a new career of writing after 50 years of science, so late in life with so little time left? Why make the effort to start fresh again? Science is your thing." Yes, that's true, but I hear, "You've had your chance. Now enjoy, relax, travel."

I prefer to think of death like those who say, "I'm *dying* to go there." Or, "I'd *die* to have that." A play on words? I suppose, but better than, "I better close up shop before I *die*."

My father had still another view of death that I call a "pretended death." His weapon: generosity. He gave away as freely as he acquired. Once, to his chagrin, he discovered that he had given his cello students, one by one, all his favorite bows, forcing him to buy replacements! "If I give it away now, then nobody waits for me to die," he said. "They inherit while I'm still alive."

I like that kind of death, a death that's not a death at all!

As for myself, I want to grow until I die, to appreciate my luck of life, for I believe, like my father did, that there is nothing better than life for us: life is just the best. I want neither a premature death nor any other type of death before my time.

One death – a final death – is quite enough for me.

TRAVELS

West Africa: Many Truths Within the Background Noise

PREPARATION: Traveling on vacation, temporarily escaping the monotony of the familiar, easing the burden of responsibilities, riding air currents far above traffic jams and local politics is intoxicating. Thus, a five-week boat tour up the west coast of Africa advertised in a National Geographic/Lindblad Expeditions catalog caught my attention a few years ago. The tour began in Cape Town, South Africa, where we would board the *Explorer,* and ended in Morocco. The journey encompassed 6,500 nautical miles. Much too long, I thought, but yet . . . the west coast of Africa? Intriguing. I toured Egypt and Morocco a few years ago – fascinating countries – but I had never visited sub-Saharan Africa, and I had never even heard of Togo or the tiny countries of São Tomé and Príncipe that were on the itinerary. Apart from its intrinsic interest and novelty – I generally prefer a fresh meal rather than yesterday's warmed-up dinner – here was an opportunity to visit the origins of some of my collected African tribal art comprising staffs, figures, metal works and textiles.

No less important, the mystique of Africa – the evolutionary birthplace of *Homo sapiens* – had a romantic flavor titillating my imagination and propensity for storytelling. I doubt that many of us from the highly developed United States, including scholars and collectors of African art, have much first-hand knowledge of this vast continent. Most tourists of sub-Saharan Africa target safaris, thinking of Africa more as a vacationland than the socially and politically complex, diverse continent that it is. The advertised *National Geographic* trip was about the culture of West Africa and included sixteen different countries (seventeen if one considered Western Sahara separate from Morocco); Nigeria, Democratic Republic of Congo, Ivory Coast, Guinea and Mauritania were skipped for safety, political or other reasons that were not revealed.

I asked my wife Lona what she thought of going on this trip.

"Africa?" Her tone said it all. "Isn't it dangerous? The newspapers are full of reports about pirates and kidnapping. Al-Qaeda. I can't keep it straight! What if we get sick?"

"The pirates are mainly along the east coast, especially Somalia," I countered, ignoring everything else. I shared her concerns, but still I wanted to go. I remembered visiting Tel-Aviv and Jerusalem, bustling with normal daily life although the Palestinians were sending rockets into Israel along the border and terrorists were sporadically bombing buses and cafes and marketplaces. Two years ago, we went to Jermaa el-Fnaa Square in the center of Marrakech in Morocco, a month after a bomb attack, yet it was crowded with peaceful activity. What to believe? What do the African newspapers report about the numerous shootings in the United States, such as the Sandy Hook school in Connecticut or in the theater in Aurora, Colorado? Would those massacres prevent an African from visiting the United States?

"I'll try to find out more about the trip," I said, sensing Lona's fears more than lack of interest. I called *National Geographic* and they told me that the better cabins were already booked although it was almost a year in advance. The popularity of the trip whetted my appetite and I figured that I'd better sign up immediately before I missed the opportunity. The lure of the hard-to-get! I felt confident that Lona would come around. In any case, it wasn't an irreversible commitment. We had five months left to withdraw without penalty. I reserved one of the available cabins on the *Explorer* and added our names to the waiting list for better accommodations, just in case one came free.

Having reservations elevated the African trip from an abstraction to a plan, and the more I thought about it, the plan boosted another notch to an adventure. It was then that I realized that this wouldn't be just another ordinary holiday but a personal challenge to re-examine my lifestyle, the values of my privileged life, and the luxury accorded by freedom and money. I have had the enormous advantages of being born in the right place and the child of the right parents. Lucky me! How about much of the rest of the world?

A few weeks later *National Geographic* called to say that they had a cancellation for one of the larger cabins. It was expensive, but I said yes. Lona was getting excited now too. Let's be comfortable, we thought, five weeks is a long stint. Interesting how a chance mailing, an impulsive reservation and a cancellation can affect one's life.

We were scheduled to explore the Atlantic coast of Africa, an area of the world I could only imagine. We got the required Yellow Fever inoculations, malaria pills, and antibiotics (just in case) as well as extras of our daily medications (cholesterol-lowering pills, blood pressure pills, vitamins) and everything else we could think of. It was as if we were heading to a different planet. It was Africa, after all, the distant land of wild animals and tribal cultures.

When the time came, we overstuffed our duffel bags with enough clothes for months, if not years, and loaded our "carry-ons" with our passports, Euros and dollars, cameras, cell phones, laptop computers, books and nooks and what-nots, and embarked into the great unknown.

WITNESSING: At first glimpse Cape Town looked like any modern city with shopping malls, residential areas, restaurants, hotels; however, waiting for the baboons to cross the street when driving to the Cape of Good Hope or stopping to gaze at the wild ostriches strolling along the beach or at penguins nesting by the roadside were outside of my ordinary experiences. My camera clicked away as if I could take the atmosphere home with me simply by capturing visual images, or perhaps I was eager to prove that I had really been there in order to add another notch to my collection of countries that I had visited.

No, my cynicism is skin-deep and shortsighted. I recognize the difference between a first-hand experience – witnessing – and a second-hand experience of reading or being told. Witnessing, in a sense, cracks open scenes just enough to let the observer slip in, if only for a few moments, and sets the imagination in motion enhancing the impact. Witnessing is analogous to showing instead of telling in a novel. Furthermore, associating what one sees with previous experiences gives it personal meaning, making the trip add to the overall structure of one's life. One might say that going on a trip is the difference between making a movie, or at least thinking about making a movie, instead of watching one. Recall for example an event that you have witnessed, such as perhaps a car accident that resulted in a serious injury. Now consider an earthquake or an act of terrorism that killed multitudes in another country that you heard about in the media. Terrible atrocities. Catastrophes and human suffering that reach us second-hand affect us, but more intellectually than emotionally. They shrink to passing flags in the parade of life, but they do not stamp indelible, lingering impressions. The power of sight – witnessing – blends one's soul with the scene. It sucks the outside in.

I felt the impact of being there when visiting Victor Verster prison in Cape Town, a minimum-security farm prison where Nelson Mandela, the great liberator and statesman, spent the last three of his twenty-seven years of imprisonment. Before that he was in the maximum-security prisons on Robben Island in Table Bay near our hotel for eighteen years and subsequently in Pollsmoor Prison in Cape Town for six years, neither of which we visited. Today Mandela's imposing statue marks the entrance to the Victor Verster prison, a paradoxical sign of honor. After it was known that he was destined to be the future President of South Africa, he was moved to a furnished house on the premises of the prison. Imagine the irony of a prisoner idolized as a symbol of hope for a better future, probably living more comfortably than the guards, and drafting the future political foundations of South Africa with President F. W. de Klerk. Even so, he was monitored continually and denied having even a family member as an overnight guest. What strange history!

Our prison guide, a long-time guard, glowed with pride as he told us how he had shaken Mandela's hand on more than one occasion when he was a prisoner. Those handshakes and few remarks that transpired between them remained a centerpiece of the guard's life even twenty-three years after Mandela's release. The universal need for a hero such as Mandela or Einstein whether in good times or bad, never ends. Regretfully, however, that need also contributes to the rise of heinous dictators such as Hitler or Stalin.

Listening to the guard talk about his experiences with Mandela, sitting in Mandela's chairs in his prison house, imagining the intangible transfer of humanity from Mandela to me through the guard's words, gave me chills and awoke an emotional response that I never would have felt if I hadn't been there. This spark of lingering hope begging to be fanned in war-torn Africa, a continent still bleeding from its many wounds that heal slowly at best, impressed me deeply.

And then there is the history of slavery when countless innocent souls, many mere children, were kidnapped and shipped like cargo to Brazil, the Caribbean islands, the West Indies and the United States. There were many sites that turned into experiences that I won't forget: Cape Coast Castle in Takoradi, Ghana (where President Obama unveiled a plaque on July 11, 2009) and the "House of Slaves" on Gorée Island in Dakar, Senegal, both World Heritage Sites; the dungeons where the captured Africans were squeezed like sardines in a can before being shipped out; the signs specifying which dungeons were for men and which for women and children (there were separate cells for women, *jeunes filles,* and children, *enfants,* in Gorée Island). The stories of slavery became palpable when I felt the heat, saw the tiny, lightless spaces hardly fit for an animal much less a human being where captives were punished for weeks and months for virtually nothing, and when I traveled the same road that the slaves trudged and circled a tree meant to "erase" their memory of home as they made their way to the Door of No Return.

I'm reminded of when I visited Alcatraz prison in San Francisco and volunteered to stay alone for less than a minute in a windowless cell used for solitary confinement that was much larger than the pitiful holes used for the African slaves. Oh, my goodness! When the door clanged shut and enclosed me in such blackness, I had no sense of whether I was in a coffin or outer space. The silence was thick and heavy. What a terrible experience! How long would I have survived as an African slave stuffed into one of their prison pits? I fear not long, but I have never been tested. Once again: lucky me! But some of the slaves did survive as nameless heroes who drifted into the mass of humanity known only as "them," those who were not born in the right place at the right time as I was. They endured great hardships and displayed enormous courage. Choice in life has its limitations. Praise or blame is not always earned to the same extent in different instances.

"G": It remains difficult to witness with objectivity not tainted by prejudice that sneaks up without warning, such as, for example, when Lona and I explored a section of Cape Town selling local carvings, textiles, jewelry and various handicrafts sprawled out on the sides of the street. Since this was our first exposure to aggressive salesmanship by the locals (which was slight compared to our experiences a few years ago in Egypt), we had no idea how tempered it was compared to what was to come in the more impoverished countries. Many items were tempting to buy, but we tried to refrain since we had a long trip ahead of us with many more opportunities. We continually said, "No, thank you, yes, the mask is very nice, but no, not now please," and so on as we made our way along the street, taking pictures as tourists do. Always taking pictures.

What pests, these salespeople, I thought, yet there was something heartbreaking about them. They seemed so earnest; their eyes were so imploring. The difficulty for them to earn a living with all the "shops" offering similar items seemed unimaginable to me. "Please, I haven't sold anything today. Only one dollar. How much will you pay? I give you good price!" A hard-core realist may not be moved by such manipulation, but I'm a soft touch. I bought textiles, a stone soap dish, a beaded necklace, a wooden salad bowl, and a few other souvenirs. I shook hands with the successful merchant after each sale, and he never failed to smile radiantly for his photograph. Was this a genuine connection or contrived? What was his economic or social status? Had I made a difference? Did he have a family or children? What were his thoughts about me, a white American tourist presumably with more money than he could imagine? Never mind. I had it all digitized in my camera!

The trouble began when I returned to the hotel carrying my purchases in several bags and sat down next to a fellow passenger and his wife in their late sixties or early seventies cooling off with beers in the air-conditioned lobby. I had not met either of them yet. Suddenly I felt self-conscious – embarrassed – that I'd bought too much, that I lacked discipline and had done something foolish that I needed to justify. I looked at my bags of souvenirs and volunteered, "I wanted to help these guys; they have so little." Did they? How would I know? What's little or much for the natives of South Africa?

After a moment the gentleman, call him G for Gentleman, said in what I discerned a judgmental voice, "You're rich; you can afford it." Harmless, certainly, and true too, as it must have been for him as well. No pauper would be on the same trip. Perhaps it was his tone, or at least how I interpreted his tone, but I found his unexpected comment strange, uncalled for and provoking. I should have brushed the comment aside with a silly response such as, "I wanted to buy a yacht, but they were sold out," or some other meaningless remark. But G's comment resonated with my age-old self-consciousness of wealth, having more than most, having more than I need. Irritated, I retorted, "How rich do you think I am?"

G answered my question with another question: "Oh, something like Rockefeller maybe?"

Why didn't I smile at my fellow tourist, who was certainly not a bad man? He knew nothing about me, or I anything about him. But a surge of anger took command of my senses, and I said, "That's a ridiculous question – idiotic – and doesn't deserve an answer!" Childish, I know. I may have been a tourist in a foreign country taking in the sights, but I was also the same person I was at home and trapped in the same brain. He didn't say another word as I chatted with his friendly wife, who seemed unaffected by the exchange.

When I related the story to Lona she said, "Good for you." I guess the person who tells a story gives it its flavor. I wonder what she would have said if G had given her his take on it.

The next day, our first at sea, G approached me on the deck of the *Explorer* and asked, "How's chemistry?" He was picking up on the brief discussion about science I had with his wife. "Fine," I said, slightly perplexed. He then laid into me saying how offensive I'd been and looking self-righteous, said, "You were a smart-ass. I just wanted you to know that." Then he went on his way. Nice start to a trip together!

Lona encouraged me to make peace with him. Good advice. When I found G alone in the lounge, I told him that I'd meant no harm and had foolishly overreacted. "Why?" he asked. I stalled for a moment. I had no easy answer. How to explain to a stranger, especially to G after our unfortunate encounters, that South Africa had triggered a guilt feeling that I needed to give to those with less than me, not only for charitable reasons, but to avoid criticism, to justify having been born lucky, to be accepted. The knee-jerk rage that conquered my common sense had resulted from witnessing events through a lens stained with my own colors. Traveling was a caged freedom that insulated me from what I saw. "Being there" was a qualified "there."

G reluctantly shook my outstretched hand, but he did not speak to me or look me in the eye throughout our five weeks together on the ship. I suppose he was in his own "there," as we all are, and which strains our efforts to truly understand and empathize. This ridiculously minor event with G, inconsequential, so potentially easy to have moved beyond, persisted like droplets of poison in the tropical air we both inhaled in the comfortable ship.

Consider now the history of the Africans and the hardships endured. They were suppressed by European colonists, sold as slaves and massacred in brutal civil wars. Now fast-forward to the present-day countries we visited, where they are striving to forgive one another to forge a peaceful future by putting the atrocities behind them. They socialize with the very people who had raped and slaughtered members of their families. Meanwhile, G and I, tourists from the developed United States, living in freedom and luxury, nurtured our grudges and struggled to even acknowledge each other. How relative it all is, and how difficult to puncture the tiny bubble in which we float.

COMPLEXITY: Most of our shipmates had traveled extensively throughout Africa and were regulars on the *Explorer* touring other places. Few failed to ask us how many trips we had taken on that ship. "This is our first," we answered. "Oh, you'll love it. We've been on seven (often more) trips," was the typical response. Professional tourists, I thought, awakening a prejudice, thinking they must be bored to death collecting destinations, exclaiming how fascinating it is, how broadening. Was it necessary to roam the world seeking interesting things,

I wondered? And then I asked myself how much experience can one truly gain by being spoon fed – entertained – by such tours, traveling in buses and peer groups and a luxurious ship? Does a spectator learn much about the animals in the zoo or experience crime watching a movie about the Mafia?

Stop! I commanded myself, knowing that my wave of negativity was paper-thin. For every argument there was a counterargument. I resigned myself to absorbing what I could. And there was much to absorb: a variety of urban and natural landscapes in the different countries (deserts, savannahs, rain forests, jungles); a sidewinder snake burrowing in the Namibian desert sand; a chameleon moving one eye at a time scrutinizing the surroundings; flamingoes feeding by the seashore; goats climbing trees (really! in Morocco); different European architectures left in place by colonists; houses in brilliant shades of primary colors; striking braided hairstyles on infants and children and young girls; women draped in dresses and men in shirts with exotic patterns in dazzling color (Africa is color!); modern sport stadiums built by the Chinese (in contrast to the limited presence of the United States); opulence and poverty side by side (more of the latter than the former); open markets; trash heaped upon trash; Africans and their families on Chinese motorcycles swarming everywhere; groups of unemployed people sitting around, drinking, speaking on cell phones, waiting (for what?); lines of empty taxis in crowded cities with not a tourist in sight (who rides in these taxis?); endless rows of shops in the open air selling trinkets, tires, used furniture (you name it); the fetish market in Ouidah, Benin selling shriveled, dead animals, skulls, bones and other magical objects of the native animist voodoo religion; hair "salons" in dilapidated shacks; signs of God and Christianity and AIDS on billboards and houses along streets needing repair and littered with potholes and gravel; rhythmic drumbeats and dancers on stilts greeting our ship at the docks and in public places; Ganvié, a fishing village built on stilts in the center of Lake Nokoué in Benin; a short trip on a pirogue (dugout canoe) up the Lobé river near Kribi, Cameroon, to see tall Bagyeli "pygmies" pretending to live in the forest for the benefit of tourists; uniformed officials boarding our ship at each port for a passport face check and eager to accept gifts; police escorts for our buses (why?). Four of our own security guards armed with rifles patrolled the ship day and night insisting there was no danger as we traveled up the coast. These are highlights.

Our voyage was as much an intensive college course as a vacation. In addition to sightseeing, we listened for hours to lectures on the *Explorer* given by hired professors and guides specializing in African history, economy, sociology and linguistics. We learned about the hundreds of languages spoken in each country, many going extinct. There were also lectures by the curator of African art in the Seattle museum, a geologist, a birder, a botanist, a biologist and an ethnomusicologist. Ambassadors to African countries, and even the former president of Ghana, J. J. Rawlings, were invited to address us on the *Explorer*, and we danced to African music with a strong South American flavor, which had been derived from slaves who had returned long ago from the Caribbean. Africa defines diversity, complexity and upheaval. It's easier to think of the stereotypical lions and giraffes grazing in fairy tale settings, and the tribes with their chiefs and hierarchy continuing their ancient customs. Those romantic aspects of Africa exist as well, adding to the scenes we observed as we tried to untangle their layered nature.

EXPECTATIONS AND BELIEFS: While the urban areas bustle with activity and cars and motorcycles and shops, rural villages of yesteryear exist a few miles beyond. We visited a Ewe village in Lomé, Togo that put on a spectacular durbar (an English word derived from an Indo-Persian term for "ruler's court") for us as they might have generations ago. This hierarchical celebration with native music and dancing had the village Chief and his Queen in the center of activities surrounded by underlings and the Chief's spokesman carrying a gold-plated staff. Royal paraphernalia reflecting wealth and status was showcased. This Chief, so important and revered in his tribe, no doubt had an ordinary position in the nearby city, perhaps in a store or as a local official of some kind. Similarly, many Africans practice an official Christian or Muslim religion in town, but then turn to their ancient native animist, voodoo religion for their private, deeper beliefs. These parallel lives with one foot in "official" customs and language (English, French or Portuguese, depending on their previous years of colonization) and one foot in their ancient, tribal traditions and native dialects add to the complexity of African society. The original, native languages of the particular cultures overlap the arbitrarily chosen borders made by colonists, creating conflict between national and tribal loyalties.

Visiting the origins of African art was one of my motivations for going on this trip. Tribal African art – incorrectly considered primitive by some – exists in museums and collections throughout the United States and Europe as extraordinary examples of artistic excellence, creative abstraction, high technical achievement and originality. African art has influenced artists worldwide, with Picasso being one of the most famous. Ethnic African art is mesmerizing. Disappointingly, however, except for some textiles, the torrent of art I saw in Africa was ordinary and stamped out for tourists, a stark contradiction to the paucity of tourists in the locations we visited. Reproductions (some very nice) abounded in shops and the streets. One gallery in Dakar, Senegal – La Galerie Antenna operated by a Frenchman (Claude Éverlé) – did have a number of excellent art pieces, but this stood alone. I bought a Nigerian stool, an Angolan stool and a Duala Cameroon staff. It seems that little of the outstanding art of sub-Saharan Africa remains in its place of origin. What sad exploitation. However, current artists continuing the tradition of imaginative and skillful expression are scattered here and there in the countries we visited, even in the impoverished townships.

Amidst all this variety and complexity, there are masses of children with smiling faces and bright eyes sparkling with life and energy. Lines of kids waved excitedly as we rode by on the train (built by the Chinese, of course) in Angola from Lobito to Benguela, as they did in the other countries. Children from a few months-old to young teenagers were in the streets, on the beach, on fences, playing with each other, being carried on the backs of their mothers or older sisters (occasionally fathers and brothers). Kids that seemed no more than eight or ten years old were fishing on their own in rickety boats (getting the evening meal?), sweeping floors or doing some other task if they were not just hanging out in groups. The children loved to be photographed and showed off for the camera. They were eager to see their images on the digital display, especially the young ones. The children are clearly a valuable resource for the future, however the sparse schools with few amenities and high expense for education create formidable obstacles.

In contrast to the children, the adults often hid from the camera or became angry if photographed. On occasion they threw rocks or sticks, protesting the invasion of their space, refusing to be treated like animals in a safari and protecting the integrity of their souls from being stolen by the camera. I found it hard not to sympathize with them, for who wants to be a spectacle for amusement? Yet, conflicted, I continued to photograph as discreetly as I could (I had a very small camera) and made an effort to communicate with them before taking their photograph or pay them to pose, although a posed image is seldom as interesting as a candid one.

Regardless of the country or the specific activity in which the children were engaged, I can't remember a child whining or appearing disgruntled. I remember only one or two instances of a baby crying. How different from the scenes I am familiar with at home, and our expectations of children in general. Expectations are critical to accomplishments as well as to what we think we ought to see. I noted myself taking an abundance of photos of townships, scattered trash, poverty, women balancing heavy loads on their heads, and tribal affairs. Was that what I expected to see? What did I miss that was hiding before my eyes, the unexpected? What would a native African choose to photograph in the United States: skyscrapers, parking lots packed with expensive cars, grocery stores?

MANY TRUTHS: As I strived to digest all this, I had to remind myself that comparing cultures, especially by a naïve tourist such as myself, is analogous to interpreting what two people speaking a foreign language are telling each other by looking at shadows of their body language. For example, these very same children that charmed me had other sides suggesting a very different story. There was an instance when I was strolling on the beach where fishermen were repairing fishing nets and tending their small canoe-like boats. I slipped, causing my hands and camera (that was more serious!) to be smeared with wet sand, so I went back to our van parked close by to get a water bottle to rinse away the muck. A small band of alert kids followed me. When I cracked open the sliding door of the van the children transformed instantly into an unruly pack heading for the van.

"Stop," I said. "What are you doing? Go away!" They ignored me as they rushed into the van, triumphantly grabbed every water bottle (nothing else) and bound out as quickly as they entered. They poured out the water, laughing, delighted with their acquisitions, and ran off. Were they going to use the empty bottles for a game of sorts, or cash them in for a few pennies? I had no idea, nor did anyone else I asked.

These nameless children are valuable resources for African nations, as are the deposits of oil and minerals, but significant obstacles exist to reduce corruption and raise the standard of living. The fates of these nations seem in jeopardy and depend on serendipity as well as education, which is replete with challenges. Tourists are among those chance events that could make a difference. Staff members on our trip brought school supplies for the children. One passenger had served as a volunteer and contributed to a hospital. Another couple on the trip had joined an organization that led to their support of a child whom they visited from time to time and whose life they enriched. Lona and I contributed to an organization that combated illegal fishing off the coast. So much more needs to be done.

Exactly what, then, was I looking at as I cruised through coastal West Africa clicking my camera here, there, everywhere that caught my attention, feeling frustrated by my inability to penetrate beneath the surface? I felt like Chevy Chase in his classic movie farce, *Vacation*, saying, "Amen, let's go," as he stands on a ridge overlooking the Grand Canyon. Perhaps when it is too overwhelming that is all one can say.

Although the trip was educational and rich with scenes for thought, I felt insulated, both physically and culturally separated from the pulse of what was there. My crossing single file across the seven canopy walkways suspended atop the rain forest in Kakum National Park in Ghana serves as a metaphor for the voyage from my perspective. Countless hidden wonders were camouflaged beneath the narrow bridges that wobbled precariously at the treetops. The landscape was picturesque and photogenic. I had the thrill of being there, smelling the fragrances, hearing the bird calls and rustle of leaves, sweating from the tropical humidity drenching my shirt, even seeing (and avoiding!) a deadly green mamba snake resting peacefully on the railing of a bridge. Yet, the high rope sides protected me from any danger of falling into the forest. The danger we feared under our conditions was as much a figment of romantic imagination as grasping the cultures and lives of the Africans was an illusion.

Whether insulated or not, real or illusory, Africa opened my eyes to how limited my experiences in life have been. Inside the mind of each stranger in the street or local guide or drummer or merchant or child or tribal chief exists a mysterious universe and network that I know nothing about, every bit as complex and interesting as my own. Janet Malcolm expressed this sentiment well in her essay, "A House of One's Own," about the Bloomsbury Group legend, Virginia Woolf: "No life is more interesting than any other life; everybody's life takes place in the same twenty-four hours of consciousness and sleep; we are all locked into our subjectivity, and who is to say that the thoughts of a person gazing into the vertiginous depths of a volcano in Sumatra are more objectively interesting than those of a person trying on a dress at Bloomingdale's?" Many truths rattle within the background noise. The challenge and reward rest in fining the ones that relate to you.

Portugal: Pausing

When I was at the Lisbon Book Festival, I went to Evora and visited the famous Chapel of Bones, which was built in the first half of the seventeenth century. Famously, the walls and columns are lined with human skulls and bones from some 5000 skeletons of Franciscan friars that had been buried in several dozen church cemeteries. Bones! Skulls! Dead people, strangers we know nothing about, who left no legacy, no heart-warming stories, no good deeds or even bad ones. And then I thought of Mozart, buried in a pauper's grave, an unmarked plot in St. Marx cemetery in Austria. How many bones of brilliant people, potential geniuses perhaps, were included among the anonymous bones in the Chapel of Bones in Portugal?

The following was posted in the Chapel of Bones by Fr. António da Ascenção (translation by Fr. Carlos A. Martins, CC):

> Where are you going in such a hurry traveler?
> Stop ... do not proceed;
> You have no greater concern,
> Than this one: that on which you focus your sight.
>
> Recall how many have passed from this world,
> Reflect on your similar end,

There is good reason to reflect
If only all did the same.

Ponder, you so influenced by fate,
Among the many concerns of the world,
So little do you reflect on death;

If by chance you glance at this place,
Stop… for the sake of your journey,
The more you pause, the more you will progress.

The last two line reached me, since they were expressing precisely what I was doing – pausing. But how was I progressing by pausing?

I reflected back a few years when I closed my research laboratory in order to devote my time to writing; I had never expected to become someone else when I retired from science. Rather, I would pause after my focus on science and obligations of employment at the National Institutes of Health for almost fifty years to explore how my experiences as a scientist might guide me to new paths and more personal discoveries. Pausing was expanding, not leaving, and it didn't require returning to the past.

I also found reading pauses in the life of writer. It was as impossible to be a writer without reading anything and every-thing that time permits as it was to be a scientist without reading the research of others. So, I read. And that's when I understood what pausing – reading, traveling, socializing – really meant. Pausing wasn't always interesting or pleasant or even helpful, but that didn't matter. Pausing was about the unexpected gems that emerge that count. I've trudged through books in which I couldn't turn the pages fast enough to finish, and others in which I strained to keep awake. But then, on occasion, from the deep abyss of the unexpected, I would read a passage so engrossing, so marvelous, that I couldn't start to write fast enough, add to or revise what I was already writing, or perhaps invent something new.

Pausing is, indeed, progressing.

Iceland: Flateyri Bookstore

We generally notice what we expect, consider what we already thought a discovery, and find experiences most satisfying when they feel familiar and touch upon our culture. When browsing in a bookstore our eyes commonly land on book covers with images that fit in some way with ourselves – perhaps a seascape for a sailor or an aesthetic composition for an artistically inclined person.

At the moment I am on an ocean cruise visiting various ports in Scotland, Denmark, Iceland, Greenland and Ireland, enjoying magnificent scenery mixed with a dash of history. Yesterday I went to one of the most beautiful fjords in Flateyri in northern Iceland. My attention focused on the vast, treeless landscape littered with waterfalls; the picturesque farms with rolls of hay wrapped in plastic sheets of various colors (each color represents a charity that will receive a percentage of the profit of sales; pink for research in breast cancer and blue for research in prostate cancer); the fjord surrounded with mountains patched with snow near the tops; and the quaint, tiny town with charming houses. The scene was as I had imagined it for a village in Iceland, but even more appealing. Drawn to the remote, I fantasized about spending a year in such a paradise to experience each season; I would read, write and explore mysteries lurking in my mind that remain buried by the torrent of distractions in my life in Bethesda.

As I strolled the main street, I saw a sign welcoming me to the "Magical World of The Oldest Original Store in Iceland". The bookstore, established in 1914, owned and run by one family for its entire existence tucked away in rural Flateyri, was a treasure hidden from the world. I went inside the small shop. Books filled shelves and tabletops. I snapped a few photographs with my trusty iPhone camera and then turned my attention to the quiet gentleman behind the cash register. His name was Eypor Jovinsson.

"This is your shop, no?" I asked.

"Yes," he said, quietly, as a matter of fact, yet I sensed a touch of pride.

He told me his great grandfather established the shop 104 years ago. Imagine how isolated it must have been then! He said that the shop was taken over by his maternal grand-mother, then his mother and now him. I forgot to ask if he had children waiting in the wings to take over from him in the future. The apartment, unchanged over the years, of Eypor's great grandparents who established the shop was attached to the bookstore. Photographs, books, a few pictures of nature, Persian rugs, an inviting chair for reading – a sequestered world – remained intact, a slice of history, a passing image of a reality worth remembering.

Accounts of business transactions throughout the shop's history lined one wall. The oldest was from 1917. The orderly, handwritten pages weren't computer printouts derived from electronics that could crash at any moment or archived in a cemetery of information due to a minor change in the operating system or glitch in the software. No, these sheets were insulated, protected from the ravishes of progress; they breathed and faded, like human beings, and would remain as a tangible lineage of a devoted family.

I gave Eypor my card with information about my memoir hoping he might want to sell it in his store, and then bought *Independent People* by Halldór Laxness. Laxness won the 1955 Nobel Prize in literature for the novel.

"Do you mind if I write a blog about your bookstore?"

"Oh, no," he responded. "It's good for business."

I loved the idea of my blog connecting Flateyri to the wide world. How different from 1914, when this small enclave stood alone and known only to a handful of local people. This thought made me appreciate the value of a single act – a family establishing a bookstore in remote Iceland that lasts generations as the world seeps in. If it's authentic, it's important. My years in science came to mind: the many times I urged young scientists in my laboratory to study what excited them, not what they thought would grab the attention of others, and ask their own questions, not only answer those of others. Perhaps 104 years later, scientists would still be reading their articles; if not, rest assured, they still had contributed a lot – they gave of themselves.

Traveling: It's about the surprise findings – the remote bookstore in Flateyri that appears like magic – the unexpected marvels that emerge when the landscape changes. Listening to these silent tunes of nature and man tells who we are and deepens our perspectives.

Greenland: Remote

Last week Lona and I were in Paamiut, and Qaqortoq. Never heard of them? Okay, neither had we. They are two small villages in Greenland, the biggest island in the world with a meager population of 56,000. The inhabitants of Greenland are confined to dots of settlements around the coast, leaving inland blanketed with glaciers – just space and more space of ice formed millions of years ago. Sadly – no, tragically – thoughtless mankind, obsessed with momentary, personal gains, does little to halt the melting of the ancient glaciers by the climate change they created.

About 1,500 people lived in tiny Paamiut. The houses sparkle in reds and blues and greens and yellows that must shimmer in the white, white snow of winter. I was dazzled by the accents of color among the rocks, and my camera works overtime. Paamiut defined "remote," as judged from my past experiences.

I was struck when our 28-year-old Inuit guide stopped to embrace his father and younger sister with a touching hug. They turned and walked away toward the sea.

"They're leaving for another village up the coast and I won't see them for eight months," he said.

They had won some sort of competition. He couldn't quite remember what the competition was about, but it didn't seem to matter. This was the winner's reward. The guide's universe was Greenland proper.

"You were born here?" I asked.

"Yes, I've been here all my life," he said. "Born and raised."

I heard my cruise peers on the tour with us say, "Can you imagine living here full time?" and "Beautiful, yes, for a few hours. But, my god, what are the winters like? What's to do?"

A few minutes later my iPhone rang. Confused, I answered the call, which had the same Maryland area code as my home. Who could be calling here?

"Hello."

My answer was a recorded message in Chinese. Could this be for real? I turned my cell phone off.

I started to notice the numerous large satellite dishes and the cranes and boats in the harbor. I saw a single taxi drive down the street but couldn't imagine where he drummed up business. I walked the whole town in less than an hour.

Our guide spoke fluent English, so I asked whether all the children were taught English.

"Yes," he said, "except those too busy playing video games on their cell phones. They don't learn it very well."

Multilingual Paamiut preoccupied with video games? Was this place really remote? Satellite dishes? Taxis? Cell phone calls from Chinese people from the United States?

Qaqortoq the next day seemed like a metropolis. The population was two to three times larger than Paamiut. A souvenir shop sold reindeer antler carvings made by a local artist. Hats and scarves made from musk ox wool – the softest, warmest wool imaginable – various other clothing items, plus assorted trinkets and knick-knacks were also for sale. There must have been more tourism here than seemed possible.

I saw a hat I might have bought, until I looked at the label: Made in China!

There was a lot of excitement in the fish market by the sea. A whale had been caught the day before and huge chunks of red whale meat were being weighed and bought. The meat looked like steak only leaner, since the blubber covers the surface of the whale rather than become integrated into the muscle.

Were these people killing whales? Yes, but very restricted. Laws were prevalent and controlling. Even tourist ships were limited in where they could stop in the small settlements in the fjords.

Our excellent guide in Qaqortoq spoke flawless English like that in Paamiut. Someone asked her where she was from.

"Southern Florida," she said. "I've been living here for eight years and love it."

A Floridian married to a Greenland Inuit guiding a Maryland resident – me. Remote was such a relative concept. To native Greenlanders, whose Inuit ancestors outlasted the Vikings and other explorers, Greenland wasn't remote at all.

I wondered what remote meant for me. I'd always thought of remote as being isolated – away from it all, where my smart phone stopped beeping and taxing my addiction to "keep in touch" with world events, where I could enter the moment. What I loved most about remote was floating in quiet, when my nerves stop jangling from incessant noises that bombarded my daily life, where I could hear a trickle in a nearby stream or a bird conveying a message in a lovely tune I couldn't decipher, where I could reflect in an indifferent world and my imagination could replace my busy life. What I called remote had all the trappings of what I imagine Greenlanders consider a busy life.

But now I wondered what had become of my concept of remote; what is remote for us earthlings these days? The

Internet has tentacles that reach everywhere, merchants tap every possible crevasse, tourists roam like locusts, leaving no corner unexplored, cell phones ring in every corner.

So, unexpectedly, Greenland broadened my concept of remote. Planet Earth seemed the last truly remote place today – anywhere on the planet – the big ball in the sky. There was no place left to hide. We are orbiting in isolation, remotely, going in circles with no idea where we are, with no hope that someone will come to our rescue. We are unreachable creatures on a tiny ball in the vast universe.

Whether in Greenland or Bethesda or elsewhere, perhaps it is time to refresh our memory of Voltaire's *Candide*, when the scholar Pangloss suggests, "..that this is the best of all possible worlds," and his student Candide answers, "…very well put… we must cultivate our garden."

Israel: Useful Junk

The mechanic had it right when he salvaged a forty-year-old car and said, "I'll keep some parts that may be useful and dump the rest." Junk – some old parts – can be useful. I felt less certain about discarding apparently useless stuff, considered junk by most people, as I sifted through the apartment of my late brother-in-law Larry, preparing it for sale. Larry, a physics professor, had passed away a week earlier of congestive heart failure. Much of what looked like junk to me didn't to him or he would have discarded it. There was the tarnished tag of his beloved golden retriever, and random newspaper clippings. I didn't know which of Larry's "junk" to keep and which to discard, because I realized that these relics were his life.

The week Larry died I was in Israel celebrating the Bat Mitzvah of my granddaughter Klara. My son Auran and his wife Tonje arranged this special trip for our whole family – both boys and their families, which, of course, included our five grandchildren. We cruised the country in a van with a guide.

I saw rusted tanks along the corridor as we traveled from Tel Aviv to Jerusalem, leftovers as reminders of Israel's 1948 war of independence. The junk tanks were historic bastions of honor that stood proud. Junk was getting increasingly hard to define, as it was for Larry's stuff.

In northern Israel we spent a day at Sde Eliyahu, an orthodox kibbutz founded in 1939 by Jewish refugees from Nazi Germany as a tower and stockade settlement. Today the kibbutz is a beautiful, thriving agricultural community pioneering organic farming. The guide stopped in front of the elementary school of the kibbutz, and what did I see? Junk: barrels, broken ladders, discarded furniture, inoperable baby strollers.

"We used to throw all this junk out," said the guide, "until we realized how useful it could be for the elementary children."

"How's that?" I asked.

"It's only junk to us, not to the kids. They use their imaginations to build structures with it. Look there, in the corner. See? It's a car with a seat and steering wheel. That's what the kid told me."

I didn't visualize the car, but that's the point. It was junk to me, but opportunity to the kid, a chance to imagine and build and play with ideas. I love it: junk as fodder for the imagination, raw material for another world. I think of giving a three-year-old boy a toy truck in a box. Excited, he rips off the wrapping, pulls the truck out of the box, and plays with the box! To the boy, the box wasn't junk. It was material for his imagination, an opportunity to see beyond the obvious, to create.

We next went to Mt. Bental in the Golan Heights, and what did we see? Metal sculptures made by Joop de Jong, a Dutch/Israeli sculptor from Kibbutz Merom Golan, lining the path to the top, made from metal remains of the Yom Kippur war of 1973 against the Syrians, creative art rising from the ashes of war rescued from discarded pieces of junk.

From Mt. Bental we proceeded to the Nimrod Fortress, the largest 13th century crusader-era castle in Israel. An earthquake in the 18th century demolished the old castle, turning it into junk of a long-gone era. Perhaps, but junk that marked history and kept the past alive. I thought of Larry's dog tag. With Larry dead, the tag became a gravestone in the cemetery of his life. I also saw the remains of a "window" in the Nimrod Fortress from which enemies could be viewed without danger as art from ruins, nothing to do with their original intent. Today the beautiful construction, some 900 years old, is a creative expression of human history. Hardly junk.

Puget Sound: Nostalgia

I'm on my way with Lona to work on my novel for three weeks at the Whiteley Center at the Friday Harbor Laboratories, a part of the University of Washington in Puget Sound. Although 47 years had passed, it seemed like recent history since I had been a Caltech graduate student on the same ferry to the Friday Harbor Laboratories to do research for my thesis. My memories and feelings from those years flooded back: the sense of freedom and adventure, the cold wind tinged with salt water, the unspoiled San Juan islands, the jellyfish near the water's surface, impervious to the passing ferry (or so it seemed), the random white caps, and the unseen drama of life and death I imagined within the sea. How I loved those days! What satisfaction to return! There was personality and vibrancy in this place.

Seeing for the second time was more than seeing twice.

Back at the research laboratories with Lona and seeing the dormitories and cabins, cafeteria, the scattered trees and rocks, the deer, foxes and raccoons roaming freely, were all present as they were before. Although a writer now, I was re-awakened by the lure of science as a force inside my mind. Colorful sea anemones, starfish, sea urchins, tunicates, sea cucumbers, barnacles, the amazing sea pens and sea feathers, looking more like plants than animals, worms, shrimps, scallops – the rich diversity of marine invertebrates and algae in the holding tanks – dazzled me, as they did before. The trickle of running seawater and the indescribable smell of a marine laboratory made me nostalgic. My sea legs of the past swayed when I saw the research vessel for collecting different species moored at the dock. My arms felt strong again when I saw the small boats I rowed while my experiments cooked that summer many, many years ago.

I was comfortable here then, like a hermit crab in a shell that fits, and I was comfortable again when I revisited a few weeks ago. I understand this way of life, the scientist's, the challenges of research, with its successes and disappointments; it's who I was and, to some extent, it's who I remain.

Or is it who I'd been, a bachelor and student 47 years ago? Now my artist wife accompanies me to make prints, collages, whatever sparks her interest, while I write. I look with pride at her accomplishments in these few weeks, another instance of my growing by association. We do not define our lives alone; we change and are each other to some extent.

Scholars – writers, scientists, movie producers – work quietly in other rooms with me at the Whiteley Center now. I see the town across the bay with its many yachts. The ferry blows its horn as it comes and goes; seaplanes skim the water as they land and leave, all as before. What's new is that I connect my laptop to the Internet, that vital link to everywhere, pull out my notes, and start to write a novel.

Write a novel! The thought jolts me still now as I reminisce. I've never done anything like that before.

Back at the Whiteley Center, I remember Van's advice. "Don't write a book," he said. "Just write whatever comes to mind. Let it flow. The connections will emerge naturally."

"Okay," I tell myself. I'll write disjointed scenes and hope they'll fuse together to create a novel. The uncertainty mirrors the mystery of life: what steers and blends our contorted paths, how much chance, how much design? And this novel I'm writing – fiction mixed with truth, about a scientist, thinly veiled as me, I fear. I've come full circle, from student to a life in science, now returning older, molding memories jumbled with new thoughts and dreams. The narrative meanders as my adventure moves along to stitch together the world of science with that of writing.

I hear, "Hello!" which startles me. Arthur Whiteley, my research mentor that summer 47 years ago, stands before me supported by a cane. Fit at 93, his eyes alert, an emeritus professor still entrenched in science, reading the scientific journals, going to seminars, discussing research with other scientists. We talk. He tells me how much he misses his wife, Helen, now dead for 20 years, and shows me photographs of her in the Helen R. Whiteley Center. Yes, that's right: *her* center, not his.

"We celebrated the tenth anniversary of the center last month," he says. "I loved creating this multicultural retreat."

I met Helen once, a fine scientist who understood that creativity shuns artificial fences. The Whiteley Center is a deserving tribute to her, but that's not my thought as I sense his pride. I think of an effacing, modest man. Once again, I see how life extends beyond one's skin: Arthur lives in Helen's Center, as her memory resides in him. And how moving that the Helen Whiteley Center, flowed from Arthur's love and not ambition, sprouting growth from mourning, and new life from death. I think of Lona and her prints – wonderful pieces of art – *my* pride in *her* work, not mine. I think of Auran and Anton, and my grandchildren, *my* genes dispersed in *them*. And then I think of my friend Van, who I visited before coming here. He escaped our way of life to a commune in the wilds of British Columbia. Although far off my traveled path, I believe a part of *me* resides with him, and, I sense, a part of *him* with me. That's how it works, whether we acknowledge it or not.

"Would you be willing to give a lecture to our students and staff on your research, although I know you're here to write?" Arthur asks.

"Of course, with pleasure," I reply.

I see my past and present merge, both alive and well, which gives me confidence.

I've reminisced enough. I'll file these memories of my trip with others in my mind and think about new adventures I hope I'll take some day.

Acknowledgements

After I closed my research laboratory at the National Institutes of Health with ambitions to write, Mia Garcia urged me to start blogging. I was tempted, but uncertain what to blog about. Margaret Dimond, an indispensable electronics helper for my ineptness at electronics, encouraged me and was setting up a website for me slanted towards writing. Thus, I followed their advice with plans to post the blogs on Facebook and my website. These blogs served as a foundation for this book.

I thank my editors, Barbara Esstman and Lucy Chumbley, for their perceptive, expert editorial comments. I have consistently learned from and taken their advice, which has invariably improved the book immensely.

I'm grateful to Bill O'Sullivan for his helpful workshop at The Writer's Center in Bethesda, which taught me the art and importance of mixing the personal with the subject matter when writing an essay.

I also thank my innumerable friends and colleagues for a lifetime of sharing thoughts.

I am grateful to Michael Kingsberry of Select Cut Media for the excellent photographs of Inuit sculptures.

I, once again, greatly thank Stevan Nikolic, the publisher of Adelaide Books, for publishing this book and for his excellent cover design and illustrations throughout the book.

Finally, as always, I thank my wife Lona for her always helpful thoughts, encouragement and patience with my long hours sequestered writing.

About the Author

During his 50-year research career at the National Institutes of Health, Joram Piatigorsky has published some 300 scientific articles and a book, *Gene Sharing and Evolution* (Harvard University Press, 2007), lectured worldwide, received numerous research awards, including the prestigious Helen Keller Prize for vision research, served on scientific editorial boards, advisory boards and funding panels, and trained a generation of scientists. Presently an emeritus scientist and writer, he collects Inuit art, is Vice-Chairperson on the Board of Directors of The Writer's Center in Bethesda. He blogs at his website (Joramp.com), has published personal essays in *Lived Experience* and *Adelaide Literary Magazine*, a novel, *Jellyfish Have Eyes* (IPBooks, 2014; Adelaide Books, 2020). He has published the following books with the present publisher, Adelaide Books: a memoir, *The Speed of Dark* (2018), two collections of short stories, *The Open Door and Other Tales of Love and Yearning* (2019) and *Notes Going Underground* (2020). He has two sons, five grandchildren, and lives with his wife in Bethesda, Maryland. He can be contacted at joram@joramp.com.

CPSIA information can be obtained
at www.ICGtesting.com
Printed in the USA
JSHW040939030721
16560JS00005B/76